Dedicated to the Sacred Heart of Jesus

Nihil Obstat: Charles W. McNamee, J.C.L.
         Censor Librorum, October 16, 2012

Imprimatur.   + David J. Malloy, D.D., J.C.L., S.T.D.
         Bishop of Rockford, October 16, 2012

Contents

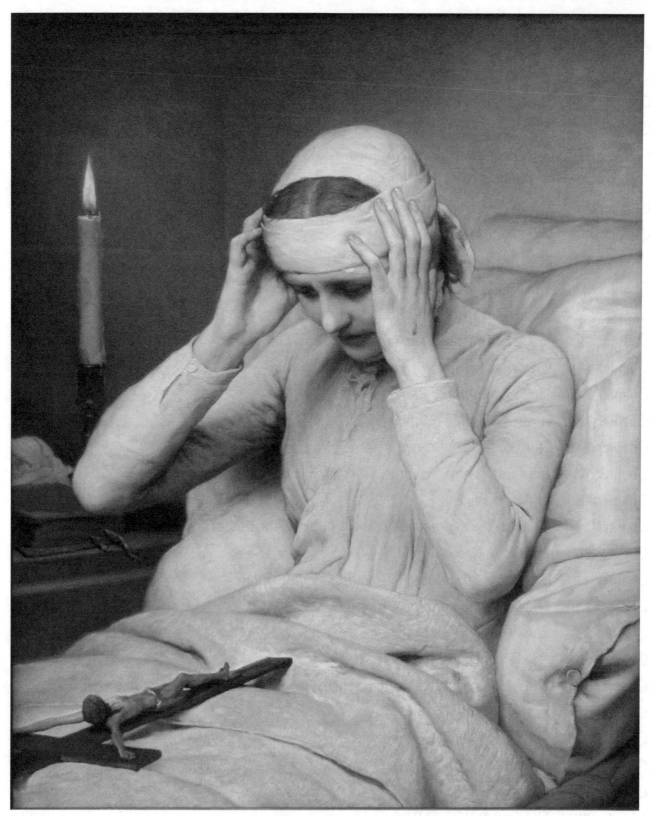

Blessed Anne Catherine Emmerich

A note on sources

Among the sources used in this history of the Bible are the visions of Blessed Anne Catherine Emmerich (1774-1824). Blessed Anne Catherine was a German Stigmatist who many believe was granted visions of Our Lord's Passion and Death. (Her visions provided the source material for Mel Gibson's movie, *The Passion of the Christ*.)

As a young girl, Anne wished to enter the convent, but had to work to support her family who were very poor. She finally entered an Augustinian convent in 1802 when she was 28. From 1802 to 1811, Anne Catherine was ill quite often and had to endure great pain. Despite being extremely frail and sickly, she performed her work cheerfully and faithfully. When Jerome Bonaparte, the ruler of Germany, closed her convent in 1812, she was forced to find refuge in a poor widow's house.

In 1813, Anne became bedridden. Soon after this, Our Lord blessed her with the stigmata, including the wounds from the crown of thorns. An episcopal commission sent to investigate her was convinced of the genuineness of the stigmata. At the end of 1818, God partially granted her prayer to be relieved of the stigmata, and the wounds in her hands and feet closed. However, the others remained, and on Good Friday all reopened.

In 1819, Clemens Brentano, a famous poet, was induced to visit Anne. She told him he was the man who was to enable her to fulfill God's command, namely, to write down the visions made to her. From 1819 until her death in 1824, Brentano visited Anne Catherine daily. He took notes of the conversations he had with Anne about her visions. He filled many notebooks with her words about scenes from the New Testament and the life of the Blessed Mother. He would write down her words, and then read what he had written back to her, making changes as necessary until she gave her approval. The result of their work was published in 1833: *The Sorrowful Passion of Our Lord Jesus Christ according to the Meditations of Anne Catherine Emmerich*.

In 1892, the Bishop of Munster introduced the process of Anne Catherine Emmerich's beatification. However, in 1928, the Vatican suspended the process when it was suspected that Clemens Brentano had fabricated and/or embellished some of the material that appeared in the book and had been attributed to Anne Catherine. In 1973, the case for her beatification was re-opened, this time focusing only on her life, without any reference to the books produced by Clemens Brentano.

Pope John Paul II beatified Anne Catherine Emmerich on October 3, 2004. The Vatican focused on her own personal holiness and set aside the books written by Brentano because "It is absolutely not certain that she ever wrote this." However, in his homily at her beatification, Pope John Paul II said, "Her words, which have reached innumerable people in many languages from her modest room in Dülmen through the writings of Clemens Brentano, are an outstanding proclamation of the Gospel in service to salvation right up to the present day."

Thus, the authors have chosen to use her visions in this history as they add depth and color to the Passion and Death of Our Lord. Those sections of the text based upon Anne Catherine Emmerich appear in italics.

Quotations and the spelling of names are from the New American Bible.

Chapter 1

Two Angelic Messages

The Annunciation

A Joyous Message

During the time that King Herod reigned over Judea, in the mountains of his kingdom, there lived two holy people: Zachary, an elderly priest, and his wife Elizabeth. Though they loved each other and had a wonderful marriage, they were sad that they had no children. They often prayed to God for a son. However, their prayers had not yet been answered.

One day, Zachary was in the synagogue, performing his duties as a priest and burning incense in the sanctuary. Suddenly, the angel Gabriel appeared at the altar. Zachary fell back in fear, but the angel told him not to be afraid. Then the angel gave Zachary some amazing news. God had heard his and Elizabeth's prayers. God would bless them with a son. They should name him John.

When Zachary heard the angel's joyous news, he could hardly believe it. In fact, he began to doubt the angel's words. He pointed out that both he and Elizabeth were rather elderly. It simply did not seem possible that at their ages they could have a baby. The angel told him that, because he doubted and had not believed God's message, he would not be able to speak until the birth of the baby. Once the angel disappeared, Zachary was unable to talk.

"Hail, full of grace, the Lord is with you."

The Annunciation

Six months after the angel appeared to Zachary, God sent the angel Gabriel with an even greater message. God sent Gabriel to Nazareth, a small town in Galilee. There, Gabriel delivered history's most important announcement to a young virgin named Mary.

Though she was a descendent of the royal family of David, Mary did not have many material goods. However, God had blessed her beyond all others in terms of spiritual wealth. It was for her surpassing holiness that God had chosen her.

While Mary was praying, the angel Gabriel suddenly appeared in her room and spoke to her. "Hail, full of grace, the Lord is with you." When Mary heard the angel's strange and startling greeting, she was troubled. She did not understand what the words could mean. However, Gabriel quickly reassured her. He told Mary that God had sent him to announce the coming of the Messiah. Gabriel told Mary that God had chosen her to be the mother of the Messiah.

When Mary heard that she was to have a baby, she was confused. She told the angel Gabriel that, although she was engaged to be married to a man named Joseph, she was still a virgin. How was it possible that she would have a child?

Once again, Gabriel relieved Mary's anxiety. He explained that the Holy Spirit would come upon her, and the power of the Most High would overshadow her, and that the Holy Child Who would be born to her would be the Son of God. Gabriel told Mary that she should name her Son Jesus. He would be the Christ, that is, the Messiah.

To prove what he said was true, Gabriel told Mary that her aged cousin Elizabeth had also conceived a child. Elizabeth was in the sixth month of her pregnancy. Anything was possible with God.

When Mary understood the incredible future that God proposed for her, she lovingly accepted the Will of God. The moment that she gave her consent to Gabriel, she became the Mother of God. In that moment, the promise that God had made to Adam and Eve in the Garden of Paradise was fulfilled: a

*"Blessed are you among women,
and blessed is the fruit of your womb!"*

woman would crush the head of the serpent. By bringing the Son of God into the world, Mary has crushed the head of Satan. With Mary's acceptance, Gabriel departed.

Mary Visits Elizabeth

The news that her cousin Elizabeth was going to have a baby filled Mary with happiness. After Gabriel left, Mary decided immediately to visit her cousin. Mary traveled quickly into the hill country to see Elizabeth.

When Mary entered Elizabeth and Zachary's home, she greeted Elizabeth. Elizabeth was at once filled with the Holy Spirit. In her womb, her unborn child leapt for joy. Elizabeth cried out to Mary in a loud voice: "Blessed are you among women, and blessed is the fruit of your womb!"

At that moment, Mary, carried away by the fullness of the Holy Spirit's grace, broke forth into the glorious song known as the **Magnificat**. Filled with grace, Mary spoke: "My soul proclaims the magnificence of the Lord, and my spirit rejoices in God my Savior; because He has looked on the humility of His handmaid. Behold, from now on all generations shall call me blessed." (For nineteen hundred years this prophecy has been fulfilled by the daily praying of the *Hail Mary*.)

Mary remained with Elizabeth for about three months. Then she returned home to Nazareth. She prepared herself for the birth of Jesus.

The Birth of John the Baptist

Shortly after Mary left, Elizabeth gave birth to a baby boy. It was the custom of the Jews to name a baby boy at his circumcision, which occurred eight days after his birth. When her friends and neighbors gathered together for the ceremony, they asked Elizabeth what name she wished for the child. She replied, "He will be called John." The relatives objected to this name saying that the baby should be named Zachary, after his father. They pointed out that no one in the family was named John.

On the tablet Zachary wrote,
"John is his name."

Then the relatives turned to Zachary. They asked him what the baby should be named. Zachary, who was still unable to speak, asked for a stylus and waxed tablet. On the tablet he wrote, "John is his name." At that instant, Zachary recovered his speech. Zachary began to praise God for all that He had done for him and Elizabeth.

Zachary and Elizabeth's relatives and neighbors were all afraid when they saw and heard what had happened. They wondered what would become of the baby who had so obviously been touched by the hand of God. Zachary prophesied that his son would be the last of the prophets. He foretold that John would prepare the way for the Messiah.

As John grew, the Holy Spirit was with him. When he became a young man, he went into the desert. There, he prayed and did penance, waiting until God called him to return to Judea to preach the coming of the Messiah to the people of Israel.

Chapter Review Fill in the blanks to complete the sentences below.

1. An angel told Zachary to name his son _____.

2. The angel _____ told Mary she would be the mother of Jesus.

3. _____ was Mary's cousin.

4. "Christ" means _____.

5. Mary's speech (song) to her cousin is called the _____.

6. Zachary prophesied that his son would be the last of the _____.

Chapter 2

Jesus Is Born

Mary wrapped her tiny Baby in swaddling clothes and laid Him in a manger.

The Dream of Joseph

When Joseph discovered that Mary was pregnant, he was very troubled. He did not understand the great miracle and the mystery in which she played so key a role. Being a good and holy man, Joseph did not want to embarrass Mary by breaking their engagement in public. So he began planning to break their engagement privately.

While Joseph was considering how to proceed, an angel appeared to him in a dream. The angel told Joseph not to be afraid to take Mary as his wife. Mary had conceived her child through the power of the Holy Spirit. Moreover, the angel said that Mary would have a Son, Whom they should name Jesus,

that is Savior, because He would save the world from its sins. When Joseph awoke, he did as the angel commanded. He married Mary.

The Birth of Jesus Christ

Soon after the marriage of Joseph and Mary, the Roman emperor, Caesar Augustus, ordered that a census be taken throughout the Roman Empire. As Judea was part of the Empire, all the Jews were required to be counted. Everyone was obliged to go to their hometown where they would register for the census. Joseph and Mary, being descendents of David, were forced to travel to Bethlehem, the birthplace of King David.

He said that they could stay in the stable behind the inn.

When Mary and Joseph arrived in Bethlehem, the city was filled with people. They could find no lodging at an inn or among their friends and relatives. Having a pregnant wife, Joseph needed to find some kind of shelter. At one inn, the kindly innkeeper had no rooms, but he said that they could stay in the stable behind the inn.

With no other choice, Joseph took Mary into the only shelter he could find: a stable. In this poor stable, among the cows and the donkeys, Jesus Christ, the Son of God, the King of Kings, was born. With inexpressible joy and loving care, Mary wrapped her tiny Baby in swaddling clothes and laid Him in a manger.

Some Shepherds Hear the Good News

On the night that Our Lord was born, some shepherds were watching their flocks in a field near Bethlehem. Suddenly, an angel appeared to them, and an intensely bright light appeared all about them. Instantly they were afraid, but the angel spoke to them,

comforting them. He told them that he had come to give them some incredibly wonderful news. The angel told them that a Baby had just been born in Bethlehem. The Baby was Christ the Lord, the Messiah, the Savior of the world. As a sign, they would find the Baby wrapped in swaddling clothes and lying in a manger. While the angel was speaking, an incredible multitude of angels suddenly appeared in the sky. They began to sing: "Glory to God in the highest and peace on earth to men of good will."

When the angels disappeared, the shepherds decided to go to Bethlehem and see the blessed Child for themselves. They hurried to Bethlehem where they found the Baby Jesus lying in a manger. When the shepherds saw Him, they told Mary and Joseph all that the angel had said about the Child. After they adored Baby Jesus, the shepherds returned to their flocks, praising God.

Eight days later, according to Jewish custom, the time came for the Baby to be named. Mary and Joseph named Him Jesus, the name that the angel had given Him before He was conceived.

Jesus Is Presented in the Temple

Forty days after the birth of Jesus, Mary and Joseph took Him to Jerusalem to present Him in the Temple according to Jewish law. They also took a pair of doves to offer as a sacrifice.

Living in Jerusalem at this time was a holy man named Simeon. The Holy Spirit had revealed to Simeon that he would not die until he had seen the Messiah. When Mary and Joseph entered the Temple with Jesus, the

Holy Spirit led Simeon into the Temple as well. Seeing the Baby, Simeon asked Mary if he might hold the blessed Child. With Mary's permission, he took Jesus in his arms and cried out his thanks to God: "Now Lord, You may let Your servant go in peace, because my eyes have seen Your salvation." Then Simeon blessed Mary and Joseph, but he warned the Blessed Mother that sorrow, like a sharp sword, would one day pierce her heart.

As Simeon was speaking, a prophetess named Anna entered the Temple. Every day she worshipped God, fasting and praying. When she arrived and saw the Baby Jesus, she too asked Mary if she might hold her Son. Anna took the Child in her arms, realizing that He was the Son of God. Then Anna went forth praising God and spreading the news of Jesus' birth to all who were looking for the salvation of Israel.

The Wise Men from the East

About two years after Jesus' birth, three Wise Men from the east came to Jerusalem asking where they could find the newborn King of the Jews. They said that they had seen His star in the east, had followed it, and had come to worship Him. When King Herod heard the words of the Wise Men he was greatly afraid. Herod called together the chief priests and his wisest counselors and asked them where the Messiah was to be born. They immediately told him that the prophets had said that the Messiah would be born in Bethlehem.

When Herod heard this report, he summoned the three Wise Men to meet with him secretly. He learned from them the exact time that the star had appeared in the east. Then Herod instructed them to go to Bethlehem to search for the Child. Herod asked them to return when they found the Child and report to him so that he could also go and worship Him.

"Now, Lord, You may let Your servant go in peace, because my eyes have seen Your salvation."

With Herod's instructions, the three Wise Men departed Jerusalem for Bethlehem. They had barely left the city when once again the star that they had been following reappeared in the sky. They began to follow it until it stopped over the house where the Child Jesus and His parents lived.

Climbing off their mounts, the Wise Men entered the home. When they saw Jesus with Mary His mother, they knelt down and worshipped Him. Then the Wise Men presented Jesus with gifts of gold, frankincense, and myrrh.

In the evening, as the Wise Men slept, God warned them in a dream not to return to Herod. Thus, they returned home by a different route. In Jerusalem, Herod waited, becoming more and more concerned with each passing moment.

The Wise Men presented Jesus with gifts of gold, frankincense, and myrrh.

Chapter Review

Fill in the blanks to complete the sentences below.

1. "Jesus" means _____.

2. After Joseph and Mary were married, _____ ordered that a census be taken all through the Roman Empire.

3. When Joseph and Mary presented Baby Jesus in the Temple, the visionaries _____ and _____ were also present.

4. Wise Men from the east followed a _____ to find Baby Jesus.

Chapter 3

The Childhood of Our Lord

The Holy Family

The Flight into Egypt

Each day that the Wise Men from the east failed to return, Herod became more and more angry. Before long, it became clear that they were not going to return and report the location of the newly born Baby. Herod went mad with rage.

King Herod, who had come to power through force and remained in power only by force, was afraid of anyone who might overthrow him. Thus, this evil and paranoid man decided to commit one of history's most atrocious acts. Since Herod did not know the exact location of the Baby Jesus, he resolved to kill the newly born King by ordering the murder of all the male babies in and around Bethlehem. It never occurred to Herod's depraved mind that God could easily protect the Baby.

While Herod prepared to commit his heinous act of mass murder against these holy innocents, an angel appeared to Joseph in a dream. The angel warned Joseph that Herod was looking for the Child in order to murder Him. The angel told Joseph to take the Child and Mary and flee to Egypt. They were to remain in Egypt until the angel told him that it was safe to return.

With a single-minded purpose and a total dedication to his family that made St. Joseph one of the greatest men to ever live, he instantly arose. Without a question or complaint, he left behind his relatives, his home, and his business. As quickly as possible he bundled Jesus and Mary onto a donkey and set out for Egypt, a land he had never been to and had barely even heard of until an angel told him to go there at once.

The Murder of the Innocents

Joseph had barely gotten his family away when Herod's minions arrived in Bethlehem. Tearing the screaming babies from their wailing mothers, the brutal soldiers callously murdered them. Pitiful weeping filled every house. The prophecy of Jeremiah had come to pass: "A sound is heard in Ramah, the sound of bitter weeping. Rachel is crying for her children, and can not be comforted, for they are dead." As these babies were murdered in place of Our Lord, the Catholic Church considers them to be martyrs and calls them the "Holy Innocents."

A few years after the murder of the Holy Innocents, King Herod died an excruciatingly painful death. After he died, Roman Emperor Caesar Augustus divided his kingdom among his three sons. Herod's son, Herod Antipater, became ruler of Galilee. Another son, Herod

Archelaus, became ruler of Judea. However, Archelaus was such a vicious ruler that his subjects appealed to Rome, and he was deposed in 6 AD.

The Return from Egypt

After King Herod's death, the angel again appeared to Joseph in a dream. The angel told Joseph it was safe to return home because Herod was dead. Once again, Joseph arose, took Jesus and Mary and returned to Israel. However, when Joseph heard that Herod Archelaus ruled Judea, he was afraid to go there. Archelaus was every bit as evil as his despicable father had been. Instead, Joseph took his family to the town of Nazareth in Galilee. Thus, what the prophets said had again come to pass: "He shall be called a Nazarene."

The Finding of Jesus in the Temple

In keeping with Jewish custom, every year Mary and Joseph traveled to Jerusalem to celebrate the Passover Feast. When Jesus was twelve years old, He accompanied His parents to Jerusalem. When the Passover celebration ended, Mary and Joseph, along with their friends and relatives, began the journey back home. However, Jesus stayed in Jerusalem.

For an entire day, Mary and Joseph traveled home. As Mary was traveling with the other women and children, Joseph thought that Jesus was with her. Mary, for her part, thought that now that Jesus was twelve, He had chosen to travel with Joseph and the men. At the end of the day, when the two groups came together, Mary and Joseph realized for the first time that Jesus was not with either group. Despite their best efforts to find Him among their friends and relatives, it was clear that He must have remained behind in

"I must be about My Father's business."

Jerusalem. Filled with the fear and anxiety that only a parent who has lost a child can experience, they rushed back to Jerusalem.

For three days, Mary and Joseph looked for Jesus, becoming more and more concerned with each passing hour. Finally, on the third day, they found Him in the Temple sitting with the Jewish teachers. Jesus was listening to them and asking them questions. All the learned Jewish leaders were amazed at his intelligence and wisdom.

When Mary and Joseph saw Jesus, they ran up to Him. Mary asked Jesus why He had not come home with them. She told Him that both she and Joseph had been frantic with worry about Him. In a kindly way, Jesus answered her that they need not have looked for Him, for He had to be about His Father's business. Mary and Joseph did not understand what Jesus meant.

Nevertheless, Jesus obeyed His parents and returned with them to Nazareth. There He grew up a loving and obedient Son. He grew older and wiser, gaining favor with both God and His fellow Jews.

Chapter Review

Fill in the blanks to complete the sentences below.

1. _____ was the ruler of Judea during the time when Jesus was a Baby.

2. The babies that were killed by this evil ruler when he tried to kill Jesus are called _____.

3. Joseph took Mary and Baby Jesus and fled to _____.

4. When Jesus was twelve years old, He was lost for three days before His parents found him _____.

Chapter 4   A Voice Crying in the Wilderness

The Holy Spirit descended in the form of a dove. A voice from Heaven spoke: "This is My beloved Son, with Whom I am well pleased."

The Preaching of John the Baptist

Jesus lived quietly in Nazareth until He was about thirty years old. An ancient tradition holds that St. Joseph had died when Jesus was about twenty. For ten years, Jesus worked in the carpentry shop making plows and chairs and caring for His mother. All the while, He was preparing for His public ministry. When the time came for Jesus to begin His public ministry, God called John the Baptist out of the desert where he had been preparing himself since his youth. John obeyed God's command and came into the area around the Jordan River.

John came out of the desert like a sandstorm, proclaiming that if the people repented and were baptized, God would forgive their sins. Soon the fame of John's preaching spread throughout the land. Great crowds of people came from Jerusalem and all of Judea to hear him preach on the banks of the Jordan River. John's message to all those who heard him was: "Do penance, for the kingdom of God is at hand." Many confessed their sins and were baptized.

John was such a powerful and energetic speaker that many people began to think that he was the Messiah. When they asked him if he was the Messiah, he told them that he was not. He told them that Another was coming Who was mightier than he. The One to come would baptize with the Holy Spirit and with fire. John was merely the voice of one crying in the wilderness.

The Baptism of Jesus

Jesus also came to John at the Jordan River to be baptized. When John saw Jesus walking towards him, he pointed at Jesus and said, "Behold, the Lamb of God, Who takes away the sins of the world." John went on to tell his listeners that Jesus was the One that he had been speaking of when he said that there was One greater than he.

When Jesus walked up to John, He asked John to baptize Him. At first, John refused, saying that he was not worthy. John said that Jesus should baptize him. Yet, Jesus said that John would be doing what God required. Thus, John agreed and baptized Jesus. Immediately, Heaven opened, and the Holy Spirit descended in the form of a dove. A voice from Heaven spoke: "This is My beloved Son, with Whom I am well pleased."

Jesus Is Tempted

After His baptism, the Holy Spirit led Jesus into the desert where the devil tempted Him. For forty days and forty nights, Our Lord fasted. Then the devil came to tempt Him. Satan tried to persuade Jesus to prove that He was the Son of God by turning stones into bread. Yet Jesus would not.

A second time, Satan tempted Our Lord. The devil transported Christ to the Temple in Jerusalem where he placed Our Lord on its highest pinnacle. Then Satan challenged Our Lord to throw Himself off the Temple. Satan said if He were the Son of God His angels would save Him. Jesus responded that it was not proper to test God.

Yet a third time, Satan tempted Our Lord. This time the devil took Jesus to a high mountain peak. There, Satan showed Jesus all the kingdoms of the Earth. Satan promised to give Jesus all these magnificent kingdoms if Jesus would kneel down and worship him. At these words, Our Lord was filled with a righteous anger. He commanded Satan to leave Him at once, saying, "The Lord your God shall you worship and Him alone shall you serve." Then Satan left, and angels came to care for Our Lord.

The Arrest of John the Baptist

The ruler of Galilee at this time was Herod Antipater. Herod, who ruled until 39 AD, had divorced his first wife and married Herodias, who had been married to his brother Philip. John publicly condemned Herod for his unlawful marriage as well as numerous other sinful activities. In fact, John had confronted Herod and Herodias in the royal palace. He told them that it was immoral for the two of them to be "married." John's words made both Herod and Herodias furious. In the hopes of silencing him, Herod had John arrested and imprisoned. However, Herod, a weak man, was too cowardly to kill John. Herodias had the nerve; she merely lacked the opportunity. Herod's birthday party presented her with her chance.

Every year on his birthday, Herod gave a magnificent banquet to honor his favorite person: himself. During his feast, Herod asked Salome, Herodias's beautiful daughter, to dance for him and his guests. Salome's dance so enthralled Herod that when she finished he promised in front of all of his guests that he would give her anything she wanted, even if she should ask for half his kingdom.

Salome, a cunning young woman, went to her mother to discuss her request. Herodias had only one desire: revenge. Herodias advised Salome to ask for the head of John the Baptist

John confronted Herod and Herodias in the royal palace.

on a silver platter. Salome returned to Herod and asked for exactly that.

Salome's request saddened Herod. Yet, because he had sworn an oath, Herod gave the order for John to be beheaded. The axe man placed John's head upon a silver platter and presented it to Salome. She took it to Herodias. Later, John's disciples came and took away his body and buried it.

Jesus Chooses His First Disciples

After His temptation, Jesus heard that John had been arrested. Jesus went to live in Capernaum, a town on the shores of Lake Galilee. One day as Our Lord was walking along the banks of Lake Galilee, two of the followers of John the Baptist, Andrew and John, saw Him. They came up and began speaking with Him and spent the remainder of the day with Him. In the evening, Andrew brought his brother Simon to meet Jesus. When Jesus saw Simon, He said, "Simon, son of John, you will be called 'Peter.'"

The next day, Jesus saw Philip and said to him, "Follow me." After Philip had listened to Jesus for a while, he went to find his brother Nathaniel. Nathaniel was sitting under a fig tree when Philip found him. Philip told Nathaniel that he had found the Messiah, Who was Jesus of Nazareth. At first, Nathaniel, who had a prejudice against Nazarenes, refused to believe his brother. However, Philip at last convinced Nathaniel to come and at least meet Jesus.

When Jesus saw Nathaniel, he commented that Nathaniel was a very honest

"Simon, son of John, you will be called 'Peter.'"

man. Nathaniel asked Our Lord how He could know anything about him, as they had just met. Jesus told Nathaniel how Philip had found him sitting under a fig tree, and how Jesus had known Nathaniel for a long time. Nathaniel was filled with awe. He proclaimed that Jesus was indeed the Son of God. Nathaniel became one of Our Lord's Apostles and became known as Bartholomew.

The Marriage in Cana

Three days later there was a wedding in Cana. Jesus and Mary attended along with Jesus' newly chosen disciples. During the wedding reception, the wine ran out. Mary came to Jesus and told Him that there was no more wine. She told Him that the newly married couple and their families would be embarrassed in front of all their friends if there was no more wine. At first, Jesus was not inclined to take any action. In fact, He told His mother that the time had not come to reveal His divine nature to the public. Yet, Mary, who knew the kindness of her Son's heart, told the servants to do as Jesus instructed.

Inside the wedding hall, there were six large stone jars of water to be used for ritual washing. Each jar held about thirty gallons of water. Jesus told the servants to fill each of the jars to the brim with water, and then to draw out the water and take it to the headwaiter. When the headwaiter tasted the water that had been turned into wine, he was astonished. He went over to the bridegroom and admonished him. He told the bridegroom that it was customary to serve the best wine first. He said that the bridegroom had kept this very fine wine for last!

This was Jesus' first public miracle. Those who saw it were astonished. They believed even more deeply that Jesus was indeed the Son of God.

[For Catholics, the wedding at Cana has a great significance. At Cana, Jesus sanctified marriage and raised it to the dignity of a Sacrament. The changing of water into wine was a precursor of the even greater change that would take place at the Last Supper when Jesus would change wine into His Blood, and the Sacrifice of the Mass when the priest changes the bread and wine into the Body and Blood of Our Lord.]

Chapter Review

Fill in the blanks to complete the sentences below.

1. When the time came for Jesus to begin His public ministry, God called John the Baptist out of the _____.

2. John began to preach in the area around the _____.

3. When John baptized Jesus, the Holy Spirit appeared in the form of a _____.

4. After His baptism, Jesus went into the desert where He fasted for _____ days and nights.

5. In the desert, the devil tempted Jesus _____ times.

6. King Herod ordered John the Baptist killed because _____ requested it.

7. Jesus performed His first public miracle during a wedding feast at _____ because of a request made by _____.

Chapter 5

Jesus Begins His Public Ministry

Jesus made a whip of cords and drove the animals from the Temple.
He overturned the tables of the moneychangers, scattering their gold and silver coins.

Jesus Chases the Moneychangers from the Temple

As the time for Passover approached, Jesus went with His mother and His disciples to Jerusalem to celebrate the Feast. However, when they entered the Temple to pray, they found that there were many vendors selling oxen, sheep, and doves. There were also a number of moneychangers sitting at tables conducting business. Filled with a righteous anger at the defilement of the Temple, Jesus made a whip of cords and drove the animals from the Temple. He overturned the tables of the moneychangers, scattering their gold and silver coins. No one dared to resist His wrath. Soon the vendors and their animals were gone.

With barely suppressed anger, the Jewish leaders asked Jesus by what authority He had driven the vendors and their animals from the Temple. Jesus' only answer to them was: "Tear down this Temple, and in three days I will build it again." The Jews were shocked. They asked how He could build a Temple in three days that had taken forty-six years and a huge amount of money to build the first time! However, they did not understand that Jesus did not mean the Temple of Jerusalem; He meant His own body.

While Jesus was in Jerusalem for the Feast of Passover, He worked several miracles. Many people who saw His miracles and heard Him speak came to believe in Him as the Messiah.

Nicodemus meets secretly with Jesus.

Nicodemus Comes to See Jesus

One night during Jesus' time in Jerusalem, Nicodemus, a member of the *Sanhedrin* (the ruling Jewish council), came to meet secretly with Him. Nicodemus told Our Lord that he knew that God had sent Him because no one could perform miracles as Jesus had done unless God were with Him. As they talked, Nicodemus asked Our Lord what he needed to do in order to be saved. Jesus answered that a person "must be born again of water and the Holy Spirit." Nicodemus did not understand what Our Lord had said. However, in response to his additional questions, Jesus merely re-emphasized what He had already said.

[It was during His talk with Nicodemus that Christ clearly taught the necessity of Baptism. The Catholic Church continues to teach this doctrine and requires all its members to be baptized. Just as the Israelites were freed from slavery in Egypt when they passed through the waters of the Red Sea, so are Christians freed from the slavery of Original Sin when they pass through the waters of Baptism.]

Jesus and the Samaritan Woman

When the Passover Feast was over, Jesus and His disciples traveled through Judea teaching and baptizing. [Only His disciples baptized; Jesus did not.] On His way to Nazareth, He came to the town of Sychar in the country of Samaria. Since Our Lord was tired, He sat down to rest near the well in front of the town's main gate. While Our Lord rested, His disciples went into the city to buy food.

As Jesus sat by the well, a woman came from the town to draw water. Jesus asked her for a drink of water. At this time in history, the Jews and the Samaritans deeply hated one another. It was unheard of that a Jew would ask a favor of a Samaritan or vice versa. Thus, when the woman heard Jesus, a Jew, ask her, a Samaritan woman, for a drink, she was quite taken aback. She asked Our Lord, how He, a Jew, would ask her for a favor – a drink of water.

Jesus replied that if she only knew Who He was, she would be asking Him for a drink. Yet, the water He would give would be "living water," and she would never thirst again. Our Lord's response caused her to ask to be given this living water. She would prefer to drink this water so that she would never be thirsty again and would not need to make the daily trip to carry water from the well to her home. In response to her request, Jesus told her to call her husband. The woman said that she did not have a husband. Then Jesus revealed that He knew all about her. He told her that she

Jesus asked her for a drink of water.

revelation caused her to think that Jesus was a prophet.

However, to test Him, the woman asked Our Lord a question. The Samaritans had built a temple on a mountain near Sychar where they offered sacrifices as the Jews did at the Temple in Jerusalem. The woman asked Jesus whether the Samaritans or the Jews were worshipping God in the right place. Jesus replied that the time had come when people would not worship God either on the mountain or in the Temple in Jerusalem. Then He told her that He was the Messiah.

When the Samaritan woman heard Jesus say He was the Messiah, she left her water jar and ran into town. She told everyone she could find that she had met the Messiah. She urged everyone to go to the well to meet Jesus. The Samaritans came to the well where they talked to Jesus. After hearing Him speak, they also came to believe in Him. They asked him to stay with them. For two days, Jesus remained in Sychar, preaching and teaching the people. As a result, many came to believe in Him.

had been "married" five times and the man she now lived with was not her husband. This

Chapter Review

Fill in the blanks to complete the sentences below.

1. The Sanhedrin was _____.

2. _____ was a member of the Sanhedrin who secretly came to see Jesus.

3. The woman that Jesus met at the well in Sychar was surprised that Jesus asked her a favor because she was a _____.

Chapter 6

St. Peter: The Fisher of Men

"Depart from me, Lord, for I am a sinful man."

Jesus Teaches in the Synagogue at Nazareth

After spending two days in Sychar, Jesus returned to Nazareth, where He had grown up. As was His custom, He went into the local synagogue to pray on the Sabbath. On this occasion, Jesus rose up to read the Hebrew Scriptures (the Old Testament) in front of the large congregation that had gathered. He was given the book of Isaiah from which He read the following passage: *"The Spirit of the Lord is upon Me; He has anointed Me, and sent Me to preach the Gospel to the poor, and to heal the contrite of heart."*

Having read the passage, Christ returned the book to the rabbis. All eyes were upon Him as He sat down. Then Our Lord told the people, "Today this Scripture passage is fulfilled in your hearing." Jesus then began to teach them and they were all astonished at His wisdom and understanding. However, they were staggered when He began to show that what the prophets had said in the scriptures about the Messiah proved that He was the One of Whom they spoke.

In shock, the people in the synagogue began to talk among themselves saying, "Is this not Jesus, the son of Joseph the carpenter?" In answer, Our Lord replied that a prophet was never honored in his own land. Jesus reminded them that the prophet Elijah was rejected by his own people. After this rejection, God sent Elijah to the country of Zarephath to aid a widow there. Our Lord also told them that the prophet Elisha had not cured any lepers in Israel, but rather a pagan named Naaman.

When the people heard these words of Our Lord and realized that He was speaking about them, they were furious! They rose up and drove Jesus out of the synagogue to the outskirts of the town. They brought Him to the edge of the mountain upon which the town was built, intending to throw Him to His death! However, when Jesus arrived at the edge of the cliff, He calmly turned and miraculously made His way through the crowd, which left Him alone.

Miracles in Capernaum

From Nazareth, Jesus journeyed to Capernaum where He went to the synagogue and taught on the Sabbath. Everyone who heard Him admired His words and His doctrines, for He taught like no other person. Jesus not only taught with authority, but the truth of His words penetrated the hearts and minds of His listeners. They knew that what He said was the truth.

One day, while Jesus was speaking in the Capernaum synagogue, a man possessed by a devil cried out, "Leave us alone! What have you to do with us, Jesus of Nazareth? Have you come to destroy us? I know you are the Holy One of God." Jesus rebuked the devil and drove it out of the man. When the people saw Our Lord's power over the devil, they were amazed. They saw that He not only taught with authority, but also had the power to command evil spirits, who obeyed Him.

When Jesus left the synagogue, He walked the short distance to the home of Peter and Andrew. (Peter's house in Capernaum was Jesus' home during much of his public ministry.) Peter's mother-in-law was quite ill with a raging fever. Her friends asked Jesus to do something for her. Our Lord approached her sickbed and took her hand. He helped her out of bed, and her fever immediately left her. Then she began to serve Jesus and His disciples food.

During the evening, the entire town gathered around the front door of Peter's home. The people brought with them anyone who was sick or possessed by evil spirits. Jesus went to the door and cured the sick and drove out many demons. The next day, Our Lord rose very early and made His way to Galilee where He again preached in the synagogues, cured the sick, and drove out demons.

The Miraculous Catch of Fish

From Capernaum Jesus made His way into Galilee and came to Lake Gennesaret. Here, a great crowd of people gathered around Him to hear Him teach. There were two boats moored alongside the lake, so Our Lord climbed into the one belonging to Peter. He asked Peter to push the boat out a little way from the shore. Then Jesus sat down and began to preach to the huge crowd.

After Our Lord finished speaking, He turned to Peter and told him to row out to the deeper water of the lake and put down his fishing nets. Peter humbly replied that he and his fellow fishermen had been out all night fishing but had caught nothing. However, because Our Lord asked it of him, he would row out and lower his nets.

No sooner were the nets over the side, before they were filled with fish! In fact, there were so many fish in the nets that the nets nearly tore apart from the sheer weight of all the fish. Peter called to his partners in the other boat to come and help him pull in the net. The other men rowed over, and soon both boats were so full of fish that they were in danger of sinking.

When Peter saw this incredible miracle, he fell on his knees at Our Lord's feet. In a trembling voice, Peter said, "Depart from me, Lord, for I am a sinful man." Yet, Our Lord's voice was filled with love and compassion

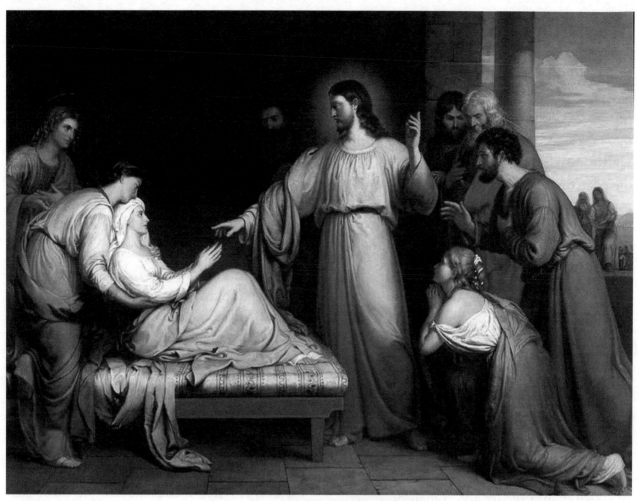

Jesus Heals Peter's Mother-in-law

when He replied that Peter should not be afraid; from now on, Peter would be a fisher of men. The men sailed their boats to the shore. There, they left their boats, their incredible catch of fish, and all their worldly possessions, and followed Jesus.

[For the Catholic, this story has greater significance than a fabulous miracle. Jesus chose *Peter's* boat from which to teach. Peter's boat is a symbol of the Catholic Church. Our Lord continues to teach from Peter's boat through the popes, the successors of St. Peter, the first pope.

Moreover, the catch of fish is itself symbolic. The lake is the world and the net is the Catholic Church. The fishermen are the priests and bishops. The fish are the faithful

who voluntarily "jump" into the Church so that they might be saved.]

Jesus Heals a Paralytic Man

One day, Jesus was teaching at Peter's home in Capernaum. Pharisees and teachers of the law who had come from all over Galilee and Judea surrounded Him, listening to Him teach. Some men carried a paralyzed friend of theirs on a stretcher to the front door of the house where Jesus was teaching in the hope that Our Lord would cure him. However, because the house was so crowded, the men could not enter with the stretcher. Determined to help their friend, the men climbed up on to the flat roof of the house. Creating an opening in the roof tiles, they lowered the paralyzed man down on his stretcher into the middle of the crowded room.

When Jesus saw the faith that the men had in Him, He said to the sick man, "Your sins are forgiven." When the teachers and the Pharisees heard these words, they became angry and accused Jesus of blasphemy. They asked themselves, "Who but God alone can forgive sins?" Jesus, Who knew what they were thinking, asked them whether it was easier to forgive a man's sins or to cure him. However, in order that they could see that He was indeed the Son of God Who had the power to forgive sins, He cured the paralyzed man. The man, who was now cured, picked up his stretcher and went home glorifying God.

This incredible miracle filled everyone who saw it with awe. They had *heard* Jesus tell the man that his sins had been forgiven, and they had *seen* Jesus cure a man who had been paralyzed. In wonder they cried out, "We have seen incredible things today!"

"Your sins are forgiven."

Chapter Review   Fill in the blanks to complete the sentences below.

1. While Jesus was in Capernaum, He healed which of St. Peter's relatives?
   _____

2. On Lake Genesareth, Jesus preached to a great crowd of people from the boat belonging to _____.

3. The miraculous catch of fish has important significance for Catholics. Peter's boat is a symbol of the _____. The lake is_____ _____ and the net is _____. The fishermen are _____. The fish are _____.

Chapter 7   The Twelve Apostles

The Sermon on the Mount

Jesus Calls His Twelve Apostles

Every day more and more people flocked to Jesus to hear His words and ask for Him to bless them and cure them of the terrible diseases that were so prevalent at this period of history. Our Lord's heart was filled with an immeasurable love and compassion for them. Seeing them milling about like lost sheep without a shepherd to guide them, He said to His disciples, "The harvest is great, but the laborers are few."

In those days, Jesus went up to a nearby mountain to spend the night in prayer. In the morning, He returned to His disciples and called them together. From among them He chose twelve whom He called His **Apostles**, which means, *sent*. Our Lord chose Simon (Peter) and his brother Andrew. He chose James (the Elder) and John, the sons of Zebedee. Our Lord also chose Philip, Bartholomew, Matthew, Thomas, James the Just or the Younger, (Jude) Thaddeus, Simon the Zealot, and Judas Iscariot.

Once Jesus had chosen these twelve remarkable men, He gave them the power to heal the sick and to work other miracles. Then He sent them forth to preach His Good News. However, He told them to take nothing with them but their walking staffs. In this way, they placed all their trust in God and had no reliance on worldly means to be successful.

Jesus warned His twelve Apostles that the path before them would be lined with suffering and end in martyrdom for most of them. They would suffer for His sake, but He too would suffer torture and death. Yet, Jesus promised His Apostles that He would always be with them. He would speak through them. Those who heard their voices, heard His voice. Those who loved them, loved Him. Those who hated them, hated Him.

Then the Apostles went forth two by two, preaching, teaching, and performing miracles. In time, Jesus added seventy disciples who were to help the Apostles in their work. The Apostles spread the word of God across the face of the Earth. Just as Gideon with his tiny band of men had overwhelmed the vast and mighty Midianite army, so too, the tiny band of Apostles defeated the powers of darkness and paganism that they encountered, bringing the Catholic Faith to every corner of the known world.

The crowd circled around Him on all sides listening in silence to His words of life. Raising His eyes to Heaven, Jesus began to speak.

The Sermon on the Mount

One day as Jesus was teaching, huge crowds from all over Judea gathered around Him, listening to Him and having Him heal them. He went up onto a small mountain with his disciples. The crowd circled around Him on all sides, listening in silence to His words of life. Raising His eyes to Heaven, Jesus began to speak.

The Eight Beatitudes

Blessed are the poor in spirit, for theirs is the Kingdom of Heaven.

Blessed are they who mourn, for they shall be comforted.

Blessed are the meek, for they shall inherit the earth.

Blessed are they who hunger and thirst for justice, for they shall be satisfied.

Blessed are the merciful, for they shall obtain mercy.

Blessed are the pure of heart, for they shall see God.

Blessed are the peacemakers, for they shall be called the children of God.

Blessed are they who are persecuted for the sake of justice, for they shall receive the Kingdom of Heaven.

The Light of the World

Shine Forth in the Darkness

After Jesus had finished speaking to the crowd about the Beatitudes, He told them that they were the salt of the Earth and the light of the world. Jesus warned them that they should not lose their flavor nor hide their light under a bushel basket. If they did this, then they were worthless. Our Lord meant that all Christians are to be strong messengers of His Word. Christians need to shine forth in the darkness of disbelief that surrounds them.

The Duties of Christians

Jesus also spoke to the crowd about the way that people should treat one another. He warned them not to act as the Scribes and Pharisees did. Rather, they should love one another as God loves them. They should love their neighbor as they love themselves and treat others as they would have others treat them. In addition to these general rules, Our Lord also gave them specific instructions.

Christ told His listeners to love their enemies and to do good even to those who hated them. They should bless those who curse them and pray for those who mistreat them. When someone hits them, they should turn the other cheek. If someone steals their coat, they should offer the thief their shirt.

The Sanctity of Marriage

Once He had spoken of the general duties of the Christian, Our Lord spoke very clearly on the sanctity of marriage. He told His listeners that people should not divorce. What God had joined together no one should put asunder.

Faith in Your Heavenly Father

Jesus also spoke to His audience about the nature of prayer. Then He taught His listeners the most perfect prayer, the *Our Father*. He told the crowd that God knows their needs before they bring them to their Heavenly Father.

Our Lord also spoke of the folly of amassing treasures on Earth. He told his listeners to lay up treasure in Heaven where neither rust nor moths could destroy them nor thieves steal them. If their treasures were in Heaven, then their hearts would be in Heaven as well.

Our Lord also instructed His listeners not to be anxious about the things of this world. "Do not worry about your life, what you will eat or drink, or about your body, what you will wear…. Look at the birds in the sky; they do not sow or reap, they gather nothing into barns, yet your heavenly Father feeds them. Are you not more important than they? Can any of you by worrying add a single moment to your life-span?"

The House Built on Rock

Jesus concluded His sermon by saying that everyone who listens to His words and acts on them is like a wise man who builds his house on a rock foundation. When it rains, and the rivers flood, and the winds blow and buffet the man's house, it does not collapse because it has been built on solid rock. Those who fail to listen to Our Lord's teachings are like a man who builds his house on the beach. When it rains, and the ocean's waves crash against this house, it is washed away because it is built on sand. There is no foundation to keep the house standing. It is little better than a child's sand castle. It collapses and is ruined.

When Jesus finished speaking, the people were greatly astonished. They were filled with admiration, not only for the content of His message, but also with Our Lord Himself. Jesus was a new experience for them. Christ taught, not as the Scribes and Pharisees, but as One having authority from God Himself.

Chapter Review Fill in the blanks.

1. Name the Twelve Apostles:

    a. _____, b. _____,

    c. _____, d. _____,

    e. _____, f. _____,

    g. _____, h. _____,

    i. _____, j. _____,

    k. _____, l. _____,

Chapter 8

Jesus Performs Many Miracles

Our Lord said, "Arise." Instantly the young man sat up and began to speak.

Jesus Heals a Leper

Although modern medicine has almost eliminated the skin disease called leprosy, during Biblical times, it was a terrible scourge. In addition to the suffering the disease caused, Jewish law required lepers to live apart from the rest of society because of the contagious nature of the sickness. Thus, they were lonely outcasts.

When Jesus came down after delivering His sermon on the mountain, a leper walked up to Him. Falling down at Our Lord's feet, the poor man begged Jesus to heal him. Jesus stretched forth His hand and touched the leper. Immediately the man was healed. Our Lord told the man to go to the Jewish priest to show that he had been healed.

Jewish law required that, when a leper was healed, he show himself to a Jewish priest. The priest would verify the cure. Once the priest examined the healed leper, the priest would then remove the restrictions which Jewish law imposed upon the former leper. This condition of the Jewish law prefigured the Sacrament of Reconciliation where the Catholic priest absolves sinners from their sins. In a very meaningful sense, the priest cleanses sinners from their spiritual leprosy.

Jesus Heals the Centurion's Servant

Shortly after Jesus had healed the leper, a Roman soldier, a centurion, approached Our Lord. The centurion told Jesus that he had a servant who was very ill and about to die. He begged Our Lord to come to his home to cure his servant. Jesus agreed. Jesus was only a short distance from the man's home when the centurion stopped Him. The centurion turned to Jesus and said, "Lord, I am not worthy to have you enter under my roof; but say only the word, and my servant shall be healed."

When Jesus heard these words from a *Roman* soldier, He was amazed. Christ turned to the crowd that was following Him and declared that He had not seen this level of faith even in Israel. Then Jesus turned to the centurion and told him, because of his faith, his servant would be cured. Immediately, the servant was cured.

The Widow of Nain's Son Is Raised from the Dead

Soon after curing the centurion's servant, Jesus, His disciples, and a large crowd traveled to the city of Nain. As Jesus strode toward the city gates, a funeral procession led by six men carrying a coffin emerged from the gates. The procession was for a widow's only son who was being carried to the graveyard. When Jesus saw the terrible sorrow of the mother, and all of her friends gathered about her, He was filled with pity. He came up to her and said, "Do not weep."

He walked over and touched the bier upon which the body lay. When He did so, the pallbearers stopped. Touching the body, Our Lord said, "Arise." Instantly the young man sat up and began to speak. Jesus gave him to his mother. When those present saw what Our Lord had done, they were filled with fear and wonder. They fell on their knees and began to glorify God, shouting, "God has visited His people." Soon this incident was reported throughout the whole of Judea and the surrounding regions.

Mary Magdalene Comes to Simon's Feast

One day, a Pharisee named Simon invited Jesus to have dinner at his home. Jesus accepted the invitation. As He was eating dinner, a woman named Mary Magdalene came to Simon's house. Mary had led a sinful life but had changed her ways. When she heard that Jesus was having dinner with Simon, she traveled to Simon's house with an ivory jar filled with expensive perfume.

Entering Simon's home, Mary Magdalene threw herself on her knees at Jesus' feet. In sorrow for her past sins, she began to weep and used her tears to wash Our Lord's feet. Then she dried His feet with her beautiful, long, flowing hair. When Christ's feet were dried, Mary Magdalene kissed them and rubbed them with the expensive perfume that she had brought with her.

When Simon saw Mary Magdalene anointing Our Lord's feet with perfume, he began to lose faith in Jesus. Simon began thinking to himself that if Jesus really were a prophet, He would know that Mary Magdalene was a well-known sinner. Jesus,

"I say to you that many sins are forgiven her, because she has loved much."

who knew what Simon was thinking, turned to Simon and asked him a question.

Our Lord said that there were two men who owed money to a banker. One man owed the banker five hundred dollars and the other owed fifty dollars. However, since neither man could repay his loan, the banker cancelled both their debts. Then Our Lord asked His question, "Which of the two men will love the banker more?" Simon replied that it would probably be the one who had the greater debt forgiven. "You are correct," said Our Lord.

Then turning back to Mary Magdalene, he said to Simon, "You see this woman? I came into your home and you gave Me no water for My feet; yet she has washed My feet with her tears, and dried them with her hair. You did not anoint My head, but she has anointed My feet. I say to you that many sins are forgiven her, because she has loved much."

Then Jesus said to Mary Magdalene, "Your sins are forgiven. Your faith has saved you; go in peace."

The Healing at the Pool of Bethesda

During the Jewish Feast of Pentecost, Jesus went to Jerusalem to attend the services in the Temple. Northeast of the Temple was a pool called Bethesda. Five porches surrounded the pool at Bethesda. Inside the porches lay a large crowd of people suffering from a variety of illnesses. At certain times, an angel would come down and touch the pool. Then, the first person to enter the pool would be cured of whatever disease he or she had.

When Jesus entered Bethesda, He saw a man who had been sick for thirty-eight years. Jesus walked over to him and asked if he wanted to be cured. The man answered that there was little chance for him to be cured because he was unable to walk to the pool himself, and he had no friends to carry him to the pool once the angel touched the waters. In response to the poor man's plight, Jesus said to him, "Arise, take up thy pallet, and walk." The man rose, picked up his pallet, and walked.

Jesus had healed the man on the Sabbath. The Jewish authorities, who were hypocrites, told the man who had been healed that it was against the law for him to carry his pallet on the Sabbath. The man replied that the One Who had healed him, had told him to carry his pallet. When the Jews asked the man who had cured him, he did not know and could not point out Jesus, Who had slipped away into the large crowd.

Later that day, the cured man met Jesus in the Temple. When the man left the Temple, he told the Jewish leaders that it was Jesus Who had cured him. Then the insincere Jews began to persecute Jesus because He had worked a miracle on the Sabbath! Jesus met their complaints by telling them that just as God the Father was at work, so too, He was at work. This response infuriated the Jews because they saw that Jesus was making Himself the equal of God. They became more determined to kill Him.

Chapter Review

Fill in the blanks to complete the sentences below.

1. The Jewish law regarding leprosy prefigured which Sacrament?

   _____

2. Jesus raised a widow's son in the city of _____.

3. Mary Magdalene washed Our Lord's feet at a feast given by _____

   _____.

4. At certain times, _____ would touch the pool of Bethesda,

   then, the first person to enter the pool would be cured of whatever disease he had.

5. Why were the Pharisees angry that Jesus had healed the crippled man at Bethesda?

   _____

   _____

Chapter 9

Jesus Teaches through Parables

The Parable of the Sower

During His ministry Jesus used short stories called **parables** to teach His listeners various religious and moral lessons. In the parables, Our Lord used *analogy*, where one thing is used to illustrate another. He showed how the people in the stories needed to behave in order to fulfill the Will of God.

The Parable of the Sower

One day, a man went out to sow grain. As he scattered the seed over his field, some fell along the path, and the birds ate it. Some seed fell on rocky ground, grew for a while, but eventually died because it lacked roots. Some of the seed fell among weeds. However, the weeds were stronger than the grain, and though both grain and weeds grew, the weeds were stronger and choked off the grain. Lastly, some of the seed fell on fertile ground where it grew and produced hundreds of stalks of wheat.

The disciples, hearing this parable, asked Our Lord what it meant. Jesus explained that the seed is the Word of God. The path are people who hear the Word, but lose their Faith to the devil, who takes it away so that they cannot be saved. The rocky ground are the people who believe but do not have true conviction and fall away easily when tempted. Those who are in the weeds have heard the Word, but as they go along in life, are choked by life's cares and its pleasures; thus, they fail to produce mature grain. However, the seed that falls on fertile soil are the people who hear and embrace the Word of God. Through hard work and perseverance, these men and women bear the fruits of the Faith.

The Parable of the Wheat and the Weeds

Our Lord told another parable about a sower. This time a man sowed good seed in his field, but as he slept, his enemy came and sowed the field with weeds. As the grain began to grow, weeds also grew among the grain. The owner of the field told his servants to let both the grain and the weeds grow together. At harvest time, the reapers would collect the grain and put it into the barns, but burn the weeds.

Jesus again explained His parable. He said that the sower is the Son of God. The field is the world. The good seed is those who have been saved. The weeds are those people who are not saved. The enemy who sowed the weeds in the field is the devil. The harvesters are the angels. At the end of time, God will send His angels out to gather everyone up. The good people will be gathered into Heaven. The evil people will be condemned to the fiery furnace where they will wail and gnash their teeth.

The Parable of the Mustard Seed

Jesus taught that the Kingdom of Heaven is like a mustard seed. The mustard seed is the smallest of all the seeds. However,

His enemy came and sowed the field with weeds.

when it grows and matures, it becomes the largest of all plants. It becomes a tree large enough for birds to nest in its branches. In this parable, Christ points to the humble beginnings of the Church, its rapid growth, and finally its ultimate glory in Heaven.

The Parable of the Pearl

Jesus also compared the Kingdom of Heaven to a merchant looking for fine pearls. When the merchant finds a pearl of great price, he sells all that he has to buy it. Jesus' message is that nothing in this world is as valuable as Heaven. Heaven is the pearl of great price for which we search during our lives. Those who have not sacrificed everything will not obtain this treasure and will realize too late how much they have lost.

The Parable of the Fishes

The Kingdom of Heaven is like a net thrown into the sea. The net catches all kinds of different fish. However, when the fishermen pull the net into their boat, they keep only the good fish. They throw away what is bad. So, at the end of the world, the angels will separate the just from the unjust.

The Parable of the Unforgiving Servant

On one occasion, Peter asked Our Lord how many times he should forgive other people. Our Lord answered, "Seventy times seven." By His response, Jesus meant that every day, Peter should forgive other people all the time. To reinforce what He had said, Jesus told His listeners a parable.

A king wished to have his subjects repay money that he had loaned them. One subject owed him ten thousand dollars. Sadly, the man did not have the money. So the king ordered that he, his wife, and his children be sold into slavery in order to pay the debt. The wretched man, hearing what was about to happen, fell upon his face before the king and begged for more time to pay. The king took pity on the man and cancelled his debt.

When the man left the king, he met a fellow who owed him one hundred dollars. He grabbed the other man by the throat and demanded he repay the money! The other man begged for a little more time to repay the loan. The first man refused and had the second man thrown into prison.

When the king learned what the ungrateful man had done, he called in the first man. The king admonished him for his cruelty. The king reminded him that his debt had been forgiven. However, as a result of his cruelty, the king threw him into prison and demanded that now he repay his debt in full. Our Lord concluded the parable by saying that God the Father would treat those who failed to forgive others as the king had treated his ungrateful subject.

Chapter Review

Fill in the blanks to complete the sentences below.

1. In His parables, Our Lord used _____, where one thing is used to illustrate another.

2. In the Parable of the Sower, the seed is _____.

3. In the Parable of the Wheat and the Weeds, the sower is _____ _____, the field is _____, the harvesters are _____.

4. In the Parable of the Pearl of Great Price, what did the merchant do?_____

_____

Chapter 10

The Master of the Wind and Sea

The Storm on the Sea of Galilee

Jesus Calms the Storm on the Sea of Galilee

After Jesus finished speaking to the people, He climbed into a boat with His disciples and told them to sail across to the other side of the Sea of Galilee. As they were sailing, Jesus fell asleep. Suddenly, a violent storm blew across the Sea of Galilee. Waves crashed over the sides of the boat, yet Jesus slept peacefully. Soon the boat began to fill with water and the disciples became afraid. With the storm increasing in ferocity, they awoke Jesus and told Him that they feared they would all drown. Then Our Lord, chiding them for their lack of faith, calmed the winds and the sea. Now the disciples were filled with awe and wonder. They said to one another, "Who is this that even the wind and sea obey Him?"

[As Catholics we know the answer to that question. The stormy sea is the world. The boat is the Catholic Church. In the Catholic Church its members safely ride out the threats and storms of the world because Jesus Christ, the Son of God, is always with us.]

Jesus Heals the Daughter of Jairus

When Our Lord's boat reached shore, a large crowd came and joyously welcomed Him. Among those in the crowd was a man named Jairus, a leader of the Jewish people. He begged Jesus to accompany him home where his twelve-year-old daughter lay deathly ill. Jesus went with him.

As Our Lord was passing through the crowd, a woman who had suffered a terrible illness for more than a decade, came up behind Him. The poor woman had sought help from numerous doctors, but they had been unable to aid her. She merely touched the hem of Our Lord's cloak and she was immediately healed. When Our Lord realized that she had touched Him, He turned to her and said, "Daughter, your faith has saved you; go in peace."

As Our Lord was speaking to the woman, one of Jairus' servants arrived with a heartbreaking message. He told Jairus that

Then Jesus took Peter, James, John, and the parents of the girl into her bedroom. Our Lord took the dead girl by her hand and said to her, "Child, arise!"

his daughter was dead. There was no longer any reason for Jesus to come to his house. However, Jesus turned to Jairus and said, "Do not be afraid; just have faith and she will be saved."

When Jesus and His disciples arrived at Jairus' home, a great crowd had gathered. Everyone was crying and mourning for the loss of such a young girl. However, Jesus told the people not to weep, for the girl was not dead, merely sleeping. At these words, the people all laughed at Him for they knew that the girl was in fact dead.

Then Jesus took Peter, James, John, and the parents of the girl into her bedroom. Our Lord took the dead girl by her hand and said to her, "Child, arise!" Immediately the girl sat up in her bed. She got out of bed and began to walk around her room. Her astonished parents rushed to her and embraced her. Jesus told Jairus and his wife not to speak to anyone about what had happened.

The Miracle of the Loaves and the Fishes

After healing Jairus' daughter, Jesus and His Apostles sailed across the Sea of Galilee to the town of Bethsaida. At Bethsaida, a great crowd gathered to hear Him. Jesus led the people out of town to a large open area where He began to teach and to heal the sick.

As the sun began to set, the twelve Apostles approached Our Lord. They suggested that He send the people home because there was almost no food to eat where they were. Jesus asked exactly how much food there was. They answered, "Five loaves of bread and two small fishes." Clearly this was not enough food to feed the crowd of five thousand men and their families.

Nevertheless, Jesus told the massive crowd to sit down in the fields. Then, He took the loaves of bread and the two fish, and looking up to Heaven, He blessed them, broke them, and gave them to His disciples to pass out to the people. When everyone had eaten their fill, the disciples gathered up the leftover food. The food that had not been eaten filled twelve wicker baskets.

When the people saw this incredible miracle, they were amazed. They began to realize that Jesus was the Messiah. Jesus knew that they were going to seize Him and try to make Him their king. Yet, this was not God's plan. So He withdrew secretly from them. During the night, He and His disciples went down to the Sea of Galilee and sailed to Capernaum.

Chapter Review — Fill in the blanks to complete the sentences below.

1. Jairus asked Jesus to heal his _____.

2. With _____ loaves and _____ fishes Jesus fed more than five thousand people and had _____ baskets of food left over.

3. After the miracle of the loaves and the fishes, Jesus slipped away quietly because He feared that _____

_____.

Chapter 11

Upon This Rock
I Will Build My Church

"I will give you the keys to the Kingdom of Heaven."

Jesus Promises the Blessed Sacrament

The day after the Miracle of the Loaves and Fishes, Jesus entered the synagogue at Capernaum. Many of those whom He had fed the day before came up to Him. He told them not to work for bread that perishes, but rather work for bread that never perishes but gives eternal life. The Son of God would give this Bread, Himself, to them.

Then Our Lord went on to explain that He was the living bread, and that this bread was His flesh. When the Jews heard His words, they were shocked. They murmured among themselves. They asked how He could give them His flesh to eat. Yet Jesus repeated even more strongly and clearly His meaning.

"Unless you eat the flesh of the Son of Man and drink His blood, you do not have life within you. For My flesh is true food, and My blood is true drink." (John 6:53-55)

For the Jews, Our Lord's teaching was very difficult to accept. Even some of His disciples who had seen His miracles and loved Him so deeply were troubled when they heard these words of Our Lord. They simply could not understand how Jesus could give them His Body to eat and His Blood to drink. Sadly, as a result of this, many of His disciples returned to their former lives and no longer accompanied Our Lord.

After some of His disciples had left, Jesus turned to His twelve Apostles -- His closest friends and supporters. To them He put the question: "Do you also want to leave?" Then Peter, the simple fisherman, who understood this incomprehensible doctrine no more than any of the others, answered Our Lord. "Master, to whom shall we go? You have the words of eternal life." Though Peter did not understand all that Christ taught, Peter was a man of faith. Jesus had said it, and Jesus had the words of eternal life. That was enough for Peter.

Peter Is Made the First Pope

Some time after this, Jesus and His Apostles came to the city of Caesarea Philippi. In order to test the faith of His Apostles, He asked them what the Jews generally thought of Him. The Apostles answered that the people held a variety of opinions. Some people thought Jesus was John the Baptist reborn or one of the Old Testament prophets. Then Jesus asked them what their own opinion of Him was. Speaking on behalf of his fellow Apostles, Peter spoke boldly, "You are the Christ (the Messiah), the Son of the living God."

When Jesus heard this plain, simple acknowledgement of His divinity, He replied, "Blessed are you, Simon. No human person has revealed this to you, but God My Father in Heaven. You are Peter (the rock), and upon this rock I will build My Church, and the gates of Hell shall not prevail against it. I will give you the keys to the Kingdom of Heaven. Whatever laws you make on Earth will also exist in Heaven."

Peter thus became the first of the Apostles to make a public profession of faith, declaring that Our Lord was in fact the Son of God and the Messiah. For his faith, Jesus made Peter the head of the Apostles and the visible head of His Church on Earth, the pope. Ever since that time, Peter's successor, the pope, has led Christ's Church, the Catholic Church.

"Upon this rock I will build My Church."

The Transfiguration

About a week after Our Lord made Peter the head of His Church, He took Peter, James, and John with Him up to Mount Tabor to pray. While Jesus prayed, He underwent a startling transfiguration. His face suddenly began to shine like the sun. His clothes became dazzlingly white. Moses and Elijah appeared on either side of Our Lord. The three men began to speak with one another.

The sight of the Transfiguration of Our Lord overcame the three Apostles. Peter, always impetuous and never shy to speak, proposed that he build three tents: one for Moses, one for Elijah, and one for Jesus. As Moses and Elijah were spirits, Peter's idea was generous but not well thought out. As Peter spoke, a cloud came and cast a shadow over them. A voice came from Heaven and cried out, "This is My beloved Son. Listen to Him."

Suddenly, Moses and Elijah were gone. Only Jesus was there with them. Our Lord told the three Apostles not to speak of their experience with anyone until He had risen from the dead. So they did not speak of the matter to anyone.

Jesus transfigured Himself with Moses and Elijah to teach the Apostles, and all His followers, a vital lesson. Moses and Elijah were the two greatest men of the Old Testament law. Moses was the lawgiver. Elijah was the great miracle worker. Christ, the Son of God, infinitely surpassed both men. He, as God, is the origin of their power. Jesus gives the new law of the New Testament. Jesus is the greatest of all miracle workers.

Moses and Elijah also represent the law and prophecy from the Old Testament. Moses appears with Jesus as a witness that He is the fulfillment of the law. Elijah bears witness that Jesus is the Messiah of Whom all the Old Testament prophets spoke.

"This is My beloved Son. Listen to Him."

Chapter Review

Fill in the blanks to complete the sentences below.

1. _____ was the first Apostle to make a public profession of faith and declare that Our Lord was the Son of God and the Messiah.

2. Jesus made _____ the visible head of His Church on Earth, the first pope.

3. The three Apostles present at the Transfiguration were _____, _____, and _____.

4. During the Transfiguration, Jesus appeared with _____ and _____ on either side of Him.

5. Why did Jesus appear with these two individuals?_____ _____

Chapter 12

A Virtuous Samaritan and a Wayward Son

The Samaritan cared for his wounds.

The Parable of the Good Samaritan

Once while Jesus was teaching, a young lawyer came up to Him. The young man asked Jesus what he needed to do in order to be saved. Jesus said, "Love the Lord, your God, with all your heart, with all your being, with all your strength, and with all your mind. Love your neighbor as yourself." The young lawyer asked Jesus, "Who is my neighbor?" In reply, Jesus told the following parable.

One day, as a man traveled from Jerusalem to Jericho, some robbers ambushed him. They stole his money and his clothes, and beat him so severely that he was left nearly dead. A short time later, a priest came down the road. He saw the beaten man lying on the side of the road, but passed by on the opposite side. A little later, a Levite passed the dying man. He also did nothing but walk past him.

However, a Samaritan man soon came upon the poor beaten fellow. The Samaritan stopped. He approached the victim and cared for his wounds. Then he put the wounded man on his donkey and took him to a nearby inn where he cared for him. The next day he gave the innkeeper some money with instructions that the innkeeper should care for the man. The Samaritan promised to pay the innkeeper any additional costs the man incurred on his way back.

When He had finished telling the story, Our Lord asked the young lawyer, "Who was the neighbor of the victim?" The young man said, "The one who showed him mercy." Jesus told him to "go and do likewise."

The Parable of the Good Samaritan and its message would have resonated deeply with Jesus' listeners. The first two characters to pass the injured man are a priest and a Levite. Neither of these two men shows any love or compassion for the injured man. Yet, both men should have known God's law by the very nature of their vocations. Sadly, they do not even show the smallest bit of human compassion.

On the other hand, the Samaritan does stop to aid the injured man. The Jews considered Samaritans to be a low class of people because they married non-Jews and did not keep all the Mosaic Law. Therefore, Jews would have nothing to do with them. [Recall the incident where Jesus spoke to the Samaritan woman at the well. Note also the response of the young lawyer, "The one who showed him mercy." The lawyer does not even want to *say* the word "Samaritan."]

In the parable, Jesus does not say whether the injured man was a Jew or Gentile.

However, it makes no difference to the Samaritan. He does not consider the man's race or his religion. The Samaritan sees only a severely injured person in need of assistance. So he helps him, more than the law or even basic human kindness demands.

The Parable of the Lost Sheep and the Good Shepherd

On another occasion, Jesus taught a lesson about His own nature. He asked His listeners, "If a man had a hundred sheep, and

"I am the Good Shepherd."

lost one, would he not leave the other ninety-nine and go look for the one that was lost until he found it? When he found it, would he not call together his friends and family and rejoice because he had found his lost sheep?" Jesus said that just as a shepherd rejoices at finding a lost sheep, so God rejoices when a sinner repents.

Jesus went on to say that He is the Good Shepherd. The good shepherd gives his life for his flock of sheep. A hired man, who works for pay, has no concern for the sheep. He flees when a wolf attacks the flock. Yet, Jesus, the Good Shepherd, lays down His life for His sheep – us.

Jesus also said that there were sheep that had not yet entered the fold. (By this Jesus meant the Gentiles.) He said that He would bring them into the fold (the Church). There would be only one fold and only one Shepherd.

The Parable of the Prodigal Son

After Jesus had explained how He was the Good Shepherd, He related a parable explaining how God the Father treated a repentant sinner.

Once there was a man who had two sons. One day the younger son asked his father for his share of the inheritance. The father gave the young man his money. With his newfound wealth, the youth traveled to a far land. Before long, the foolish young man had wasted the money on evil companions, gambling, alcohol, and drugs. When his wicked companions discovered that he had run out of money, they abandoned him. He was reduced to miserable poverty.

Faced with starvation, the foolish young man went to work for a farmer, feeding the man's pigs. The pigs grew fat on the husks of corn that they ate. The young man longed to eat the pigs' food, but no one offered him any. Soon, the young man came to his senses. He realized that the workers on his father's estate led better lives than he was now living. He rose up and decided to return home. He knew he was not worthy to be called his father's son, but he hoped that at least his father would give him a job.

While he was still a long way from his father's house, his father saw him. His father rushed out to meet him. His father hugged and kissed him and welcomed him home. This prodigal son, who had spent his inheritance so recklessly and wastefully, was deeply ashamed. He told his father that he had sinned against him and Heaven, and for that he no longer deserved to be called his son.

However, his father loved his wayward son. The father ordered his servants to put the finest shoes and clothes on him. He told them to put a gold ring on his finger. Then the father told his servants to kill a fattened calf to celebrate his son's return.

Meanwhile, the elder son had been out working in the fields. As he was walking home, he heard music and dancing and laughter. As he neared his home, a servant came out to tell him what was happening. When he learned the cause of the celebration, he became very angry and refused to enter the house. His father came outside to plead with him to join the party.

Yet, the elder son refused to go into the house. He told his father that he had not

His father hugged and kissed him and welcomed him home.

been disobedient nor led an evil life wasting away his inheritance. In fact, he had been an excellent son who worked hard every day. Yet, his father had never thrown him and his friends a party. Why was it when his disobedient younger brother returned, did he deserve a party?

The father said that all that he owned belonged to the older son. However, he told his older son that they should rejoice because his brother was dead and had come back to life. He had been lost and was now found.

In this parable, Christ beautifully teaches the doctrine of Penance or Reconciliation. First, the prodigal son recognizes that he has sinned. Then, he repents and returns to his father. Next, he confesses his sins and is ready to do penance for what he has done.

In the same way, the repentant sinner examines his conscience. He recognizes his sins, repents, and confesses his sins to a priest. The priest imposes a penance, which the repentant sinner accepts. The priest absolves the sinner, who is then reconciled to the Lord.

The Parable of Lazarus and the Rich Man

Jesus told another parable to His listeners. There once was a very rich man who dressed in expensive clothes, lived in a huge mansion, and ate the finest food. Outside the mansion's gate, there lived another man. His name was Lazarus. He was a homeless man covered in sores. Every day Lazarus would go to the back door of the mansion and beg for scraps of food. At night, dogs came and licked his sores.

In time, both Lazarus and the rich man died. Angels carried Lazarus to the bosom of Abraham. The rich man had a wonderful funeral and was buried. Sadly, the rich man went to Hell.

In Hell, the rich man looked up and saw Lazarus and Abraham. The rich man called up to Abraham. He begged Abraham to let Lazarus dip his finger in water and drip the water on his tongue, for the flames of Hell burned him.

In response, Abraham reminded the rich man that during his life he had been given all of life's good things while Lazarus had received none of them. Now Lazarus enjoyed all that was good while the rich man suffered. Abraham also told the rich man that a great chasm existed between those in Hell and those with Abraham. None could cross that chasm. Even if Lazarus desired, he could not drip water on the rich man's tongue.

Finally, the rich man appealed to Abraham on behalf of his five brothers. He asked that Lazarus be sent to warn them so that they did not end up in Hell. Abraham refused. He told the rich man that his brothers had Moses and the prophets. If they did not listen to them, then they would not listen even if a man were to rise from the dead.

Chapter Review

Fill in the blanks to complete the sentences below.

1. Jesus told the Parable of the Good Samaritan to answer the question _____ _____.

2. The Good Shepherd gives _____ for His flock of sheep.

3. Jesus said that just as a shepherd rejoices at finding a lost sheep, so God rejoices when _____.

4. In the Parable of the Prodigal Son, Christ teaches the doctrine of _____.

5. In the Parable of Lazarus and the Rich Man, what happened to Lazarus when he died? What happened to the rich man when he died?

_____

_____

Chapter 13

Jesus Has Dinner with Mary and Martha

Mary Magdalene sat at Our Lord's feet listening to Him speak.

Jesus in the Home of Mary and Martha

After Jesus had been traveling for a time, He came to the town of Bethany. Mary Magdalene and her sister, Martha, lived in Bethany. They welcomed Jesus and His Apostles into their home.

In order to show the proper respect for her guests, Martha worked around the house, cleaning and preparing food. On the other hand, Mary Magdalene sat at Our Lord's feet listening to Him speak. After a while, Martha asked Jesus if He would please tell Mary to help her serve the dinner. Yet, the Lord replied that Martha was worried about too many things. He told her that only one thing was needed. Mary had chosen the right thing, and He would not take it from her.

Through Mary and Martha, Our Lord teaches two key lessons to Catholics. First, Catholics need to be concerned more with the things of the next world than of this world. Martha represents the material world, while Mary represents the Heavenly Kingdom. Jesus chides Martha for worrying about the things of this world, rather than the one thing that matters — the salvation of her soul.

The second lesson Catholics should learn is the respect for women that Jesus has in this episode. In Jesus' time, men treated women like Martha. They were expected to cook and clean. They would not have been invited to listen to the men speaking. Yet Jesus invited Mary Magdalene to sit at His feet along with His Apostles. Jesus has an attitude toward women that is at odds with the prevailing sentiment of the time. These days, as her enemies attack the Church for being "anti-woman," the falseness of that attack is plainly evident by the words and actions of Our Lord.

Jesus Heals a Man Born Blind

One day as Jesus was walking along, He saw a man who had been born blind. His disciples asked Him who was to blame for the man being born blind. Was he to blame or was it his parents? Jesus answered that the blindness was not the fault of the man or his parents. The man had been born blind so that God's power might be shown in Our Lord.

Jesus went up to the man and spat on the ground. He mixed His spit with the dirt to make mud. Then He rubbed the mud on the man's eyes. Our Lord told the man to wash his face in the Pool of Siloam. The man obeyed. He went, washed, and returned able to see.

When the people who knew the man saw him, they were shocked. They asked him how it was that he could see. The man told them that Jesus had cured him. Then they took the man to the Pharisees. The Pharisees asked the man how he had gained his sight. Once again the man replied that Jesus had healed him.

It would seem that a miracle that healed a blind man would fill a person with awe and wonder. However, Jesus' miracles just caused the Pharisees problems. In this instance, Jesus had cured the blind man on the Sabbath. A miracle performed on the Sabbath created discord among the Pharisees. Some Pharisees said that Jesus could not be from God because he performed a miracle on the Sabbath! Others answered that a sinner could not perform a miracle. Others believed that a simpler explanation was that the man

Jesus rubbed mud on the blind man's eyes.

had never been blind but had been faking. In order to find out whether the man had been blind all his life, the Pharisees sent for his parents.

The parents of the formerly blind man told the Pharisees that he was their son and that he had been born blind. However, they had no idea how he was able to see or who cured him. The parents told the Pharisees to talk to their son as he was old enough to speak for himself. The man's parents said these things because they feared the Pharisees, who, everyone knew, hated Jesus.

The Pharisees recalled the man who had been healed. He answered their questions, but they did not like his answers. When he tried to reason with them, pointing out that only someone who comes from God could perform such a miracle, the Pharisees became very angry. They kicked him out of the synagogue.

When Jesus heard that the man had been cast from the synagogue, He went to find him.

Jesus asked the man if he believed in the Son of Man. The man asked who the Son of Man was so that he could believe in Him. Jesus replied that He was the Son of Man. The man fell to his knees and said, "I do believe, Lord."

The Ten Lepers

As Jesus was making His way to Jerusalem, He met ten lepers on the outskirts of a village. According to Jewish law, lepers were required to live apart from the rest of society. The ten lepers shouted to Jesus to have pity on them. Jesus told them to go and show themselves to the priests. As they ran to the priests, they were cured.

One of the men, realizing that he had been cured, returned. He threw himself down at Jesus' feet and began to adore Our Lord. Jesus asked the man what had happened to the other nine men. Were they not also cured? Then Jesus said to him, "Stand up and go; your faith has saved you."

Chapter Review

Fill in the blanks to complete the sentences below.

1. When Jesus visited Mary and Martha's home in Bethany, _____ worked around the house, cleaning and preparing food, while _____ sat at Our Lord's feet listening to Him speak.

2. Which of the sisters represents the material world? _____

3. Which sister represents the Heavenly Kingdom? _____

4. What can we learn about Jesus' attitude toward women from His relationship with Mary and Martha? _____

_____

Three Memorable Parables

"For everyone who exalts himself will be humbled.
Those who humble themselves will be exalted."

The Parable of the Pharisee and the Tax Collector

Jesus told this parable to those who were sure of their own goodness and despised everyone else.

Two men went to the Temple to pray. One man was a tax collector; the other man was a Pharisee. The Pharisee stood apart from everyone else and prayed, thanking God that he was not like the rest of humanity – greedy and dishonest. He especially thanked God that he was not a tax collector. Meanwhile, the tax collector stood in a back corner of the Temple. His head was bowed. He struck his chest saying, "O God, be merciful to me, a sinner."

Jesus told His listeners that the tax collector went home justified while the Pharisee did not. "For everyone who exalts himself will be humbled. Those who humble themselves will be exalted."

The Rich Young Man

One day as Jesus was teaching, a rich young man approached Him. The man knelt before Our Lord and asked what he had to do in order to be saved. Jesus told him to obey the Ten Commandments. The young man said that he had obeyed the commandments since he was a young child.

Jesus turned to him and told him that he needed to do one more thing. He should sell all that he had, give the money to the poor, and come follow Our Lord. At these words, the young man went away in sorrow, for he was very wealthy. After he had left, Jesus turned to His disciples. Looking at His disciples, Jesus remarked that it was very difficult for a wealthy person to enter the Kingdom of Heaven. The disciples were astonished but Jesus told them that with God's help, all things were possible.

The Parable of the Laborers in the Vineyard

In his Gospel, St. Matthew relates one of Our Lord's most interesting parables. St. Matthew is the only Evangelist to do so.

Jesus said that the Kingdom of Heaven is like a landowner who, at 6 a.m., goes out to hire men to work in his vineyard. The owner agrees to pay the workers a full day's wage for the day's work. Then the men start working.

At 9 a.m., noon, 3 p.m. and 5 p.m., the owner of the vineyard visits the marketplace. He sees men standing around not doing anything. So he tells these men to go work in his vineyard and, at the end of the day, he will pay them what is just.

At 6 p.m., the owner calls all of the workers together. He pays those that had started at 5 p.m. a full day's wage. When the

Jesus told the rich young man that he needed to do one more thing.

workers who had started working at 6 a.m. also receive a full day's wage, they begin to complain. They had expected to receive more. They point out to the owner that he paid men who had only worked for one hour the same amount of money as he had paid them. They had worked a full day. They felt they deserved more.

The owner replies that he has paid them the amount that they had agreed to. He has not cheated them. Besides, is he not allowed to do as he wishes with his own money? Are they complaining that he is being unjust, or that he is being generous?

There are many levels of meaning in this parable. It is notable that St. Matthew is the only Evangelist to relate this story. Matthew was a tax collector. As such, the vast majority of the Jews considered him a public sinner. Thus, in their minds, he would be excluded from Christ's vineyard. Yet, Our Lord invited him to become an Apostle. Our Lord is also teaching that everyone can be saved, even at the last minute. The parable also teaches that the reward for those who labor their entire lives and for those who come to the Lord even at the moment of death, will be eternal life.

Chapter Review
Fill in the blanks to complete the sentences below.

1. What lesson did Our Lord teach with the Parable of the Pharisee and the Tax Collector?_____

2. What advice did Jesus give to the rich young man?

3. The Parable of the Laborers in the Vineyard only appears in _____ Gospel.

4. What is Our Lord teaching with the Parable of the Laborers in the Vineyard?

Lazarus, Come Forth!

"Lazarus, come forth!"

The Death and Resurrection of Lazarus

While Jesus was teaching along the banks of the Jordan River, He received word that Lazarus, the brother of Martha and Mary Magdalene, was very ill. Jesus loved the two sisters and their brother Lazarus, so Mary and Martha thought that Our Lord would hurry to Bethany to heal Lazarus. Yet for two days, Jesus failed to set out for the home of His friends. Finally, He told His disciples that they should go to Bethany. Along the way, Jesus told his disciples that Lazarus had died.

When the group arrived in Bethany, Martha met Our Lord, but Mary remained at home. Martha complained that Jesus had arrived too late to save Lazarus. However, Jesus told her that Lazarus would rise.

Martha sent word to Mary that Jesus wished to speak with her. Mary left her house and went to meet Jesus who was still on the outskirts of the village. When Mary saw Jesus, she fell at His feet and told Him that, if He had arrived sooner, Lazarus would not have died.

When Jesus saw Mary and all the people who had come with her, He was deeply troubled. He asked where they had buried Lazarus. When they took Him to the tomb, Jesus wept. Our Lord lifted up His eyes to Heaven and cried out in a loud voice, "Lazarus, come forth!" Immediately, Lazarus rose and came out of the tomb. Lazarus was wrapped in burial clothes, so Jesus told the onlookers to unbind him.

Many people had accompanied Mary and Martha to the tomb. When they saw this incredible miracle, they began to believe in Jesus. However, some of them went to the Pharisees and told them what Our Lord had done.

The Plot to Kill Jesus

When the Pharisees heard that Jesus had raised Lazarus from the dead, and that more and more Jews were following Him and His teachings, they were incredibly concerned. The Pharisees feared that if they left Jesus alone, all the Jewish people would begin to follow him. In the past, men claiming to be the Messiah had proven to be false. However, these false Messiahs had caused the Jewish government to become unstable. The Pharisees feared that if a large number of Jews followed Jesus, they would push Him to become a political leader. Then He would lead them to rebel against the Romans who occupied their country. Rome would crush the rebellion. The Romans would take away the Pharisees' religious and political authority. They worried that the Jewish nation would cease to exist.

The Pharisees turned to Caiaphas, the high priest. They asked him what he thought of this issue. Caiaphas responded that it was better for one man to die rather than the entire Jewish nation. Then, as High Priest, Caiaphas prophesied that Jesus would die for the Jewish nation.

From that moment, the Pharisees planned to murder Jesus. For this reason, Jesus no longer walked openly among the people. He left Bethany with His disciples and traveled to the town of Ephraim.

Clearly, the Pharisees cared nothing for the truth of Jesus' message. They hated Him because more and more people had begun to follow Him. These men were so hungry for power, that they simply ignored the fact that Jesus had raised a man from the dead! In fact, they even plotted to kill Lazarus as well.

Caiaphas and the other Pharisees plot to kill Jesus

Barren of any spiritual beliefs, all that concerned the Pharisees was the power of Rome.

Zacchaeus Climbs a Tree to See Jesus

A few days after raising Lazarus from the dead, Jesus arrived in Jericho. In Jericho, there lived a man named Zacchaeus, the head tax collector. As Jesus passed through the city, Zacchaeus tried to catch a glimpse of Our Lord. However, Zacchaeus was rather short, so he could not see above the heads of the crowds.

Since Zacchaeus knew the route Our Lord was taking, he ran ahead and climbed a sycamore tree. When Jesus came to the sycamore tree, He looked up and saw Zacchaeus. He told Zacchaeus to come down because He wanted to spend the day at Zacchaeus' house. Zacchaeus hurried down and welcomed Jesus into his home with great joy.

When the people saw that Our Lord had entered Zacchaeus' house, they began to grumble. Jesus had gone into the house of a tax collector whom they all believed to be a public sinner because of his profession. Yet Zacchaeus told Our Lord that if he ever cheated anyone, he would repay the amount four times over. Jesus said to Zacchaeus, "Today salvation has come to this house."

"Zacchaeus, come down."

Chapter Review

Fill in the blanks to complete the sentences below.

1. Lazarus was the brother of _____.

2. Historically, false Messiahs had caused the Jewish government to

   _____.

3. The Pharisees feared that the Romans would take away their _____

   _____.

4. As he was short, _____ climbed a sycamore tree to see Our Lord.

Our Lord's Last Days

The people praised Jesus as He rode into Jerusalem.

Mary Magdalene Again Anoints Jesus

As had become His custom, six days before Passover, Jesus returned to Bethany to stay with Mary Magdalene, Martha, and Lazarus. On this occasion, Simon the leper gave a supper for Our Lord. Among the guests was Lazarus. Martha helped serve the food. As everyone was eating dinner, Mary Magdalene came into the dining room. Mary had a large bottle of very expensive perfume. As she had done several months before, she poured the perfume onto Jesus' feet and then used her long hair to dry them.

Judas Iscariot, one of the Apostles, asked Our Lord why the expensive perfume had not been sold. Judas said that the proceeds from its sale could have fed many poor people. He said this, not because he cared about the poor, but because he was a thief. He held the Apostles' money and stole what was given to them. So Jesus responded, "Leave her alone. You always have the poor with you, but you do not always have Me."

The Entry into Jerusalem

The next day, the large crowd that had attended Simon's banquet came out to meet Jesus as He entered Jerusalem riding a young donkey. The people spread their cloaks and palm branches on the ground before Our Lord. As Jesus rode into Jerusalem, the people blessed and praised Him. Meanwhile, the Pharisees, who had already decided to kill Jesus, became even more upset that the people were praising Our Lord as the Messiah.

Jesus Again Drives the Moneychangers from the Temple

As was His custom when He was in Jerusalem, Jesus went to the Temple. As He entered the Temple Porch, He saw people buying and selling their animals, and exchanging money. He made a whip out of rope, and with it, drove these people from the Temple.

Once the Temple had been cleansed, Jesus began to teach to great throngs of people. People also brought Him the sick, the blind, and the lame. Our Lord cured them all. When the Pharisees saw how excited and awed the people were by Christ's words and His works, they were even more indignant than before.

The Parable of the Wedding Feast

The next day Jesus was teaching in the Temple. Once again, He used a parable to explain an important point. Jesus said that the Kingdom of Heaven is like a king who threw a wedding feast for his son. The king sent his servants to tell the guests about the feast, but they refused to come. A second time the king sent his servants to the guests with the invitation to the feast, but instead of coming to the banquet, they seized the servants and killed them. When the king learned that his servants had been murdered, he sent his army to punish the killers.

In order that there would be guests at the prince's wedding feast, the king sent his servants out into the streets of his kingdom. The servants were instructed to invite everyone they could find to come to the wedding banquet. The servants did as the king commanded and soon the banquet hall was filled with guests.

When the king entered the banquet hall, he saw a guest who was not appropriately dressed for the feast. The king asked the man why he had not worn a wedding garment. However, the man did not answer. The king then ordered his servants to tie the man up and throw him outside into the darkness where he would grind and gnash his teeth.

Jesus concluded His parable by saying that many are called, but few are chosen.

[To the modern American reader this parable might seem unfair. After all, the king had told his servants to go out into the streets and find men and women to attend the wedding feast. How could this poor man have been expected to come to a wedding banquet already appropriately dressed? Yet, in the East during Jesus' time, it was the custom for kings to provide guests with wedding clothes. The crime of the man who was cast out was that he had failed to put on the clothes that the king had provided to him. Jesus' listeners would have known this.]

"Give to Caesar"

The Pharisees, who heard the parable of the wedding feast, knew that Jesus meant that they were the guests who refused to come to the feast. They began to plot how they could trap Jesus with His own words. Then they would have an excuse to have Our Lord condemned to death.

In the hope of tricking Jesus, the Pharisees sent some of their followers, as well as some of King Herod's friends, to speak with Jesus. These men began by flattering Our Lord. They praised Him for His courage in telling the truth without concern for what other people might think. When they thought that they had deceived Jesus, they sprung their "trap." They asked Him whether it was lawful to pay taxes to Caesar, the Roman Emperor, or not.

The Pharisees thought that this tax question was incredibly clever because there was no answer that Jesus could give that would not cause Him harm. If He answered "yes," then the Jews would hate Him for supporting the Romans who occupied their country and mistreated them. On the other hand, if Our Lord answered "no," King Herod would have Him arrested as a revolutionary who opposed the government. The Pharisees were certain that their cunning plan had trapped Our Lord.

"Give to Caesar the things that are Caesar's, and give to God the things that are God's."

However, Jesus knew of the Pharisees' evil plan. Jesus demanded that His questioners show Him the coin with which the taxes were paid. When they gave Him the coin, He asked them whose image was impressed upon it. They replied, "Caesar's." So Jesus said to them, "Give to Caesar the things that are Caesar's, and give to God the things that are God's."

When the plotters heard Our Lord's answer, they were amazed. Not daring to ask Him any more questions, they went away. Clearly, they were not as cunning as they thought!

Jesus Foretells the Destruction of the Temple

After Jesus finished speaking to the agents of the Pharisees and King Herod, He and His disciples left the Temple. As they were walking out, some of the disciples began to admire the beauty and magnificence of the Temple. They commented on how large and imposing the building was. Jesus told them not to be too impressed by the Temple. He told them that, before long, the Temple would be completely destroyed. (Of course Our Lord was correct. In 70 AD, a Roman army under the command of Titus destroyed the Temple.)

Chapter Review — Fill in the blanks to complete the sentences below.

1. Why was Judas upset that Mary Magdalene had used expensive perfume on Our Lord's feet? _____

2. In the Parable of the Wedding Feast, who are the guests who refuse to come to the feast? _____

3. In the Parable of the Wedding Feast, what did the man the king had thrown out do wrong? _____

4. What did Jesus say when He was asked whether it was lawful to pay taxes to Caesar? _____

5. When was the Temple destroyed? _____

Chapter 17

Ten Girls, Three Servants, Two Parables

The Parable of The Wise and Foolish Girls

The Parable of the Wise and Foolish Girls

Once there were ten girls in a wedding party who took their oil lamps and went out to meet the bridegroom. Five of the girls were wise, but the other five were foolish. The foolish girls took only the oil in their lamps. The wise girls carried extra oil for their lamps with them.

The bridegroom was delayed, and the girls became tired as they waited for him. Before long, they had all fallen asleep. Late at night someone shouted that the bridegroom was coming up the road. The ten girls arose and prepared to meet him. However, the foolish girls did not have enough oil for their lamps, and the lamps went out. They asked the wise girls for a portion of their oil, but the wise girls said that they only had enough for their own lamps. The wise girls told the other girls to go to the store to buy more oil.

While the foolish girls were at the store buying oil, the bridegroom arrived. The five girls who were ready went into the wedding feast with him. Then the doors were shut behind them.

When the foolish girls returned, they found the doors to the wedding hall locked.

They knocked and begged for the doors to be opened. Sadly, the bridegroom refused to let them enter. He told them that he did not know them.

Jesus concluded His parable by warning His listeners always to be ready, for no one knows the day or the hour when the Son of Man shall come.

The Parable of the Three Servants

Once there was a man who was going on a long journey. He called together his servants and put them in charge of his property. He divided his property according to the ability of each of the three servants. He gave five gold coins to one, two gold coins to another, and one gold coin to the last. Then he left on his trip.

The servant who had received the five coins invested them wisely and made five more coins. The servant who received two coins also doubled his money. However, the servant who had received the one coin buried it in his yard.

When the man returned from his trip, he met with his servants. The first servant brought forth the ten coins. When the man saw that his money had been doubled, he thanked his servant. He told the servant that because he had been faithful in managing a small sum, he would be given a larger sum. His master invited him to share in his happiness.

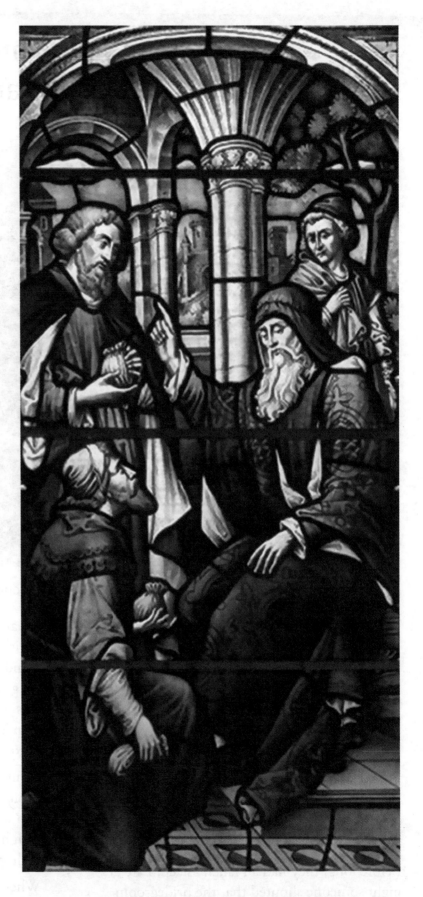

The Parable of the Three Servants

Then the servant with the four coins entered. Likewise, his master congratulated him on doubling his money. He too was promised greater tasks. He was also invited to share his master's happiness.

Finally, the servant who had buried the coin came before his master. The servant told his master that he knew that the master was a hard man. So he buried the money in the ground out of fear. The master yelled at him for his laziness. He took the gold coin and gave it to the servant who had the ten. Then he ordered that the lazy servant be tied up and thrown outside into the darkness.

The Parable of the Three Servants is one of Our Lord's most meaningful. Once again Jesus is teaching His listeners how to live and prepare for the day when we stand in judgment before Him. Our Lord makes the point that, while not everyone starts off the same, He expects that whatever gifts are given to each person be used by them to the best of their abilities.

Our Lord is also addressing the nature of the relationship that we should have with God. The first two servants have faith in their master. For that reason they believe and trust in him. As a result, they seek to do his will. They use the gifts he has given them for good to produce greater value.

On the other hand, the third servant is motivated by fear. He lacks faith, which makes him spiritually deaf and blind. As a result, he is paralyzed into inaction. He chooses to neglect his spiritual gifts, which he hides away. The lazy servant has not even tried to do his master's will. As a result, his master throws him into the darkness.

Chapter Review

Fill in the blanks to complete the sentences below.

1. In the Parable of the Wise and Foolish Girls, what did the wise girls do, and how did this differ from the foolish girls? _____

   _____

2. What message did Jesus teach in the Parable of the Wise and Foolish Girls? _____

   _____

3. In the Parable of the Three Servants, what does the servant who received one gold piece do with it? _____

4. What motivates the three servants? _____

   _____

5. In the Parable of the Three Servants, Jesus is teaching His listeners how to live and prepare for _____.

Chapter 18

Holy Thursday

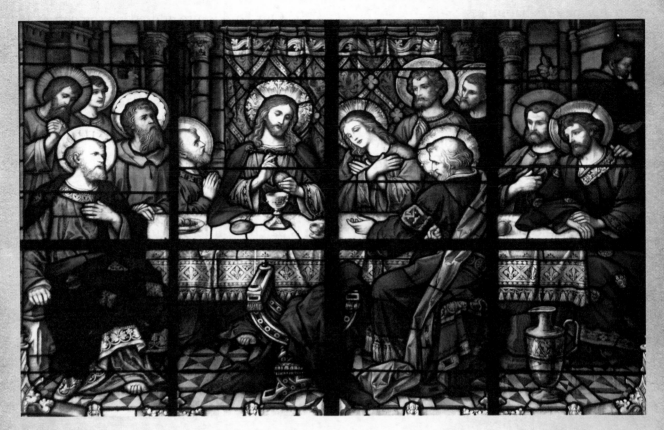

The Last Supper

The Last Supper

On the first day of Passover, Jesus sat down to dine with His twelve Apostles. Our Lord told them how eager He was to have this last meal with them before He suffered and died.

When the meal was over, Jesus rose from the table. He wrapped a towel around His waist and poured water into a washbasin. He began to wash His Apostles' feet and dry them with the towel. When Our Lord came to Peter, Peter declared in his humility that he would never allow Jesus to wash his feet! Jesus replied that Peter did not understand what Jesus was doing, but that he would later. Our Lord also said that if Peter did not allow Him to wash his feet, then Peter could no longer be His Apostle. At these words, Peter, always impetuous, but filled with a deep burning love for Our Lord, told Jesus that He should wash his hands and his head too!

When Jesus had finished washing His Apostles' feet, He sat back at the dinner table. He explained to them why He had washed their feet. He said that the servant is not greater than the master. He told them that, as He had washed their feet, they should also wash the feet of one another. Jesus had given them an example to follow.

In teaching the necessity of washing the feet, Jesus was really teaching the necessity of the Sacraments of Baptism and Reconciliation. These two Sacraments "wash" away sin. Christ washed His Apostles' feet at the Last Supper as a symbol of these two Sacraments.

The Institution of the Holy Eucharist and Holy Orders

Jesus returned to the table and took the bread that was on the table in front of Him. He blessed the bread, broke it, and gave it to His Apostles saying, "Take, eat, This is My Body which is given for you." By these words Our Lord changed the bread into His most Holy Body.

After the Apostles had eaten, Jesus took the cup of wine. Again He gave thanks, blessed the wine, and gave it to His Apostles saying, "Drink of this all of you; this is the Blood of the New covenant. It shall be shed for you and for many for the remission of sins. Do this in memory of Me." With these words Our Lord changed the wine into His most Precious Blood. Thus, He instituted the Holy Eucharist.

At the same time, Jesus also instituted the Sacrament of Holy Orders. When He said, "Do this in memory of Me," He empowered the Apostles as priests to consecrate the bread and wine into His Body and Blood just as He had done. Thus, Our Lord ordained His Apostles as the first priests and bishops of the Church. They would go forth to ordain other priests and bishops who would celebrate the Mass until the end of time.

Judas, the Betrayer

After Our Lord had turned bread and wine into His most Precious Body and Blood, Jesus became very sad and troubled. He knew that one of His beloved Apostles had made a deal with the Pharisees to betray Him. In fact, Judas Iscariot had agreed to betray Jesus for thirty pieces of silver. Even after receiving the Eucharist, Judas, who for a year had been a thief, was still going to betray Our Lord. With a heavy heart, Jesus declared, "One of you is going to betray Me." Instantly, there was an uproar among the Apostles. Each began to ask Our Lord, "Is it I?"

John, the Apostle Jesus loved most of all, was sitting next to Our Lord. Peter motioned to John to ask Jesus of whom He spoke. John obeyed Peter's direction and asked Jesus, "Who is it, Lord?"

Jesus answered, "I will dip some bread into the bowl of oil and give it to the man." Then Our Lord dipped the bread into the bowl and handed it to Judas Iscariot. As soon as Judas ate the bread, Satan took possession of him. Jesus told Judas to do what he was going to do quickly. None of the other Apostles knew what Jesus meant when He spoke to Judas. Judas was in charge of the money, so they thought that Jesus was telling Judas to buy some food or give some money to the poor. After Our Lord spoke to him, Judas went out to betray Our Lord to His mortal enemies.

Jesus Predicts That Peter Will Deny Him

After Judas left the room, Jesus said that the time had come for the Son of Man's glory to be revealed. God's glory would be revealed through Jesus. Jesus told His Apostles that He would not be with them much longer. When Our Lord said this, Peter asked Jesus where He was going. Jesus answered that where He was going Peter could not now follow, but could follow later. Peter became very excited and asked, "Lord, why can't I follow you now? I am ready to die for you!"

Jesus turned to the great-hearted and always impulsive Peter. With sadness in His voice, Jesus told Peter that that night, before the rooster crowed, Peter would deny Him three times. Peter said that even if he had to die with Christ, he would not deny Him. All of the Apostles agreed with Peter that they would die before denying Our Lord.

Judas leaves to betray Our Lord.

Christ's Promise of the Holy Spirit

After Judas had left and Christ had spoken to Peter, He turned to the Apostles. He told them that they should love one another as He loved them. He promised that God the Father would send the Holy Spirit to guide them and the Church through the rest of history. Jesus concluded by offering a prayer for them and for all who came to believe in Him.

Chapter Review

Fill in the blanks to complete the sentences below.

1. Which of the Apostles initially refused to let Our Lord wash his feet? _____

2. In teaching the necessity of washing the feet, Jesus was really teaching the

   necessity of the Sacraments of _____.

3. What two Sacraments did Jesus institute at the Last Supper?

   _____ _____

4. At the Last Supper, Jesus said that Judas would _____, and

   Peter would _____.

Jesus Is Arrested and Taken before the Sanhedrin

Chapter 19

As Jesus suffered in the garden, an angel came to strengthen and fortify Him.

The Agony in the Garden

Jesus left the supper room with His eleven Apostles and began to walk to the garden of Gethsemane. Jesus and His Apostles had lately spent several nights in the garden. The garden was large, surrounded by a hedge, and contained a few fruit trees.

It was about nine in the evening when Jesus entered the garden. When the twelve men walked into the garden, Jesus told His Apostles to sit down and rest. He took Peter, James, and John with Him deeper into the garden where He looked for a place to pray. As He left to pray, Jesus turned to the three Apostles. He instructed them to pray. Leaving these three Apostles behind a little ways, Jesus stepped into the wildest part of the garden

to pray. He walked down the hill to a small grotto, where hanging plants screened Him. There, He knelt down in prayer.

Overwhelmed with sorrow, Jesus fell on His face on the cruel ground. All the sins of the world, past, present, and future, crushed down upon Him. Lifting up His eyes to Heaven, He offered up a prayer to God the Father. He offered Himself to God as the sacrifice to atone for the sins of all of mankind.

As Our Lord continued to pray, the terrible weight of the sins of the world bore down on His soul. His anguish was so great that He cried out, "Father, if it is possible take this cup of suffering from Me. However, not My Will, but Thy Will be done." As Jesus prayed, a long beam of light came out of Heaven. Inside that light was an angel who came to strengthen and fortify Our Lord.

Trembling, Jesus rose. It was about 10:30 as He made His way to the place where He had left Peter, James, and John. As He approached them, He could see that they had fallen asleep. Overwhelmed with grief and anxiety, they could not remain awake. Jesus folded His hands together and fell down on His knees beside them. He shook them awake and asked why they were sleeping. He asked why they could not watch one hour with Him. When they saw Our Lord's haggard face, John asked if he should leave and call the other Apostles. Yet Jesus answered that they must remain. Peter, James, and John had seen the Transfiguration; now they had to witness Our Lord's agony in the garden. Before He left, Jesus again warned them to stay awake and pray with Him.

Once again Jesus returned to the grotto to pray as He had done before. After about an hour of prayer, He returned to His Apostles who again had fallen asleep. For a third time, Jesus returned to the grotto to pray. As He had done the previous two times, He asked that the cup of suffering be taken from Him. However, He remained obedient to the Will of God the Father.

So intense was the struggle that took place in Our Lord's human nature, which recoiled at the terrible sufferings He knew He would soon undergo, that from every pore of His holy body, large drops of bloody sweat burst forth. These large drops ran down Our Lord's face. His hair became matted together.

The blood became entangled in His beard. When this bloody agony had ceased, He rose up and walked back to His Apostles.

At Jesus' approach, Peter, James, and John woke from their sleep. They barely recognized Our Lord. In the moonlight they saw a man Whose face and beard were covered in blood. His clothes were also stained with blood. Our Lord told them to arise. The moment had almost arrived when He would be delivered into the hands of His enemies.

The Kiss of Judas

There is no reason to believe that when Our Lord chose Judas to be one of His twelve Apostles, that Judas was not totally devoted to Jesus. Jesus loved Judas as He did all the Apostles, and repeatedly tried to turn him from his path of treachery when Judas began to change. Sadly, it seems that Judas had never understood Our Lord's message. Judas expected Jesus to establish an earthly kingdom and to give him an important role in His government. When that had not happened, Judas became disgusted.

Judas also saw that Our Lord and His followers were being subject to greater and greater persecution. Thus, Judas sought to make friends with Our Lord's enemies. These men were in positions of power. They could reward Judas with money and power – something that Jesus was not going to give him.

For many months, Judas had stolen the money with which the other Apostles had entrusted him. Nevertheless, his greed and desire for power cannot be the sole motivations for committing history's most heinous crime. There was an evil at work more deep and sinister than simple greed. It appears that Judas had come to hate Jesus. In fact, St. Luke writes that Satan had "entered into" him. It appears Judas wanted to get rid of Our Lord and so accepted a token payment.

On the Wednesday before Holy Thursday, Judas attended a secret meeting with the members of the Sanhedrin who most hated Our Lord. At this meeting, held in the house of the high priest, Caiaphas, Judas agreed to betray Jesus for thirty pieces of silver – the price of a slave. The plan was for the Sanhedrin's men, the Temple guards, to arrest Jesus in a private place where no friendly crowd would defend Him.

After Judas left the Last Supper, he hurried to the Pharisees to finalize the scheme to seize Our Lord. Judas planned to enter the garden of Gethsemane at the head of the Pharisees and their soldiers. He would approach Jesus and embrace and kiss Him as if he were His friend and Apostle. The kiss would identify Jesus and be the soldiers' signal to seize Him. The Pharisees, who did not trust Judas, told their soldiers to keep close to him. They had already paid him and were afraid he would run off with their money. In any event, once Judas betrayed Christ, they were

The Kiss of Judas

not going to have any more to do with the treacherous wretch.

The Sanhedrin took no chances with their plan to arrest Jesus and subdue His eleven exhausted Apostles. Against Jesus and His eleven men they sent what they believed was overwhelming force. Several hundred men, including Temple guards, accompanied Judas. The Temple guards carried swords, some carried clubs, and others carried torches. A few Pharisees also went with Judas and the soldiers. In addition, more than one hundred fully armed Roman soldiers also were sent to arrest Jesus.

Jesus was speaking with His three Apostles when Judas and his small army of men came into the garden. When the other eight Apostles saw Judas and his heavily armed gang, they hurriedly joined Our Lord, Peter, James, and John. When Judas saw Jesus, he swiftly walked up to Him, said "Hail, Rabbi," and kissed Him.

Then Jesus walked over to the gang of men and in a clear voice asked them whom they were seeking. The leader of the soldiers answered, "Jesus of Nazareth." Jesus replied that He was the one they sought. Our Lord had barely finished speaking when the soldiers were thrown back as if by an invisible hand.

Our Lord Is Arrested

As they lay on the ground, Jesus reproached the soldiers. He scolded them saying, "You have come with swords and clubs to arrest Me as if I were a robber. Every day I sat teaching in the Temple, yet you did not arrest Me." At these words, the soldiers arose and hesitantly edged up to Jesus.

Peter, brave and impetuous, saw the soldiers about to arrest Jesus. Peter drew his sword, swung wildly, and cut off the right ear of Malchus, the high priest's servant. Malchus grabbed his head and fell to the ground bleeding. After Peter struck Malchus, Jesus told him to put away his sword. He told Peter that those that live by the sword would die by the sword. Christ also told Peter that if He asked, God the Father would send twelve legions of angels to defend Him. Jesus walked up to Malchus and healed his ear.

At this point, Malchus disappears from recorded history. However, some traditions hold that Malchus was instantly converted by Our Lord's miracle. During Our Lord's Passion, he carried messages from the Blessed Mother and Our Lord's friends.

After Jesus had healed Malchus, the soldiers seized Our Lord. The Apostles, seeing Our Lord's arrest, fled into the night. Peter and John followed behind the soldiers at a distance.

The soldiers tied Our Lord's hands as tightly as possible. Then they tied a rope around His waist so that they could drag Him. Jesus had bare feet so they dragged Him down the worst roads with sharp stones. As the group reached the bridge over the Kedron River, the soldiers brutally struck Our Lord. The force of the blow knocked Him off the bridge into the water. The soldiers dragged Him from the river on the other side. All the way to the house of Caiaphas, the high priest, the soldiers, and the Pharisees beat Jesus with knotted ropes.

Jesus before the High Priest

Finally, the gang led Jesus to Caiaphas' house. There, the chief priests, elders, and the Pharisees had gathered. Caiaphas sat in the center of a raised platform. The seventy members of the Sanhedrin, the Jewish ruling council, sat around him. As it was about three o'clock in the morning, he had been waiting for many hours for Our Lord to be brought before him, so he was very angry. Their goal was to find evidence so that they could put Jesus to death – a goal they had long ago agreed upon.

Jesus was led across the courtyard into the council chamber. The moment that Our Lord was brought into the room, Caiaphas began to scream at Him. Caiaphas questioned Our Lord about His teachings. However, Jesus stood silently before him, looking down. Our Lord's silence infuriated Caiaphas and the soldiers, and the soldiers struck Our Lord in an attempt to force Him to answer Caiaphas.

Next, Caiaphas called for witnesses to testify against Jesus. The first witnesses were people of low quality, and their testimony was so poor, that even Caiaphas could not understand it. Then Caiaphas called upon the Pharisees. These men tried to speak calmly, but their hatred for Our Lord could be seen on their faces and heard in their voices. However, even the Pharisees could not get their stories straight. Each one contradicted the one who spoke before. Even though all these people came forward to lie, Caiaphas and the Sanhedrin could not find any

Jesus stood silently before Caiaphas.

evidence they could use to have Our Lord executed.

Finally, two witnesses came forward to testify that Jesus had said that He could tear down the Temple and rebuild it in three days. Caiaphas demanded that Our Lord answer this latest charge. Still, Jesus remained silent.

Our Lord's silence had a dramatic effect upon the onlookers. It made Caiaphas and many of his followers indescribably angry. Yet, the quiet dignity of Our Lord as He endured insults and punches touched the hearts of many of those in attendance.

By now Caiaphas' anger was out of control. The soldiers struck Our Lord again and again in order to force Him to answer the high priest. Finally Caiaphas said, "I order you to tell us under oath before the living God whether you are the Messiah, the Son of God." For a moment it appeared that Jesus would not answer. Then, in a majestic voice that carried over the shouts of the crowd, Jesus replied, "I am."

When Caiaphas heard Our Lord's reply, he tore his robes. He screamed, "He has blasphemed!" Caiaphas declared that they had all heard the blasphemy so there was no need for any more witnesses. Under Jewish law, the penalty for blasphemy was death. Thus, Caiaphas called out to the Sanhedrin, "What is your opinion?" Having gathered for the purpose of condemning Jesus, their unanimous opinion was: "He deserves to die!"

Chapter Review

Fill in the blanks to complete the sentences below.

1. Jesus left eight of the Apostles near the entrance to the garden of Gethsemane, but took _____ with Him deeper into the garden to pray.

2. In the garden, the struggle that took place in Our Lord's human nature was so intense that _____.

3. Judas had never understood Our Lord's message; rather, he had expected _____ _____.

4. What evidence is there that Judas was not motivated solely by greed in betraying Our Lord? _____

5. Judas kissed Jesus in order to _____.

6. Defending Jesus, Peter drew his sword and cut off the right ear of _____.

7. At this time, _____ was the High Priest.

8. The Sanhedrin convicted Jesus of the crime of _____.

Chapter 20

The Cock Crows

In shame, Peter recalled Our Lord's words, "Before the cock crows..."

Peter Denies Our Lord

Meanwhile, Peter and John had followed the soldiers when they took Our Lord before Caiaphas. In disguise, Peter and John had entered the courtyard. Nicodemus, a member of the Sanhedrin, had let them into the council chamber. There, they saw all that happened to Our Lord.

When Our Lord told Caiaphas that He was indeed the Messiah, Peter and John could no longer endure the sight of our suffering Lord. They left the room. John went to tell Mary that her Son had been condemned to death. However, Peter could not bring himself to leave Our Lord. Thus, he remained in the courtyard.

Peter, who had spent his life dragging fishing nets into his boat, was a large, burly man. He also spoke with a Galilean accent. Though in disguise, his size and accent could not really be hidden.

Peter approached the fire around which the soldiers and some other people were sitting and talking, and staying warm on the cold night. Peter was silent and clearly upset. His attitude made the others suspect that something was wrong.

A maid came over to the fire and saw Peter. She said that he had been with Jesus. Her words startled Peter. Frightened, surrounded by enemies, literally in the camp of his enemies, Peter denied knowing Our Lord.

Peter stood and walked away from the fire. As he walked away, another woman noticed him. She told the people that were with her that Peter was one of Christ's disciples. When questioned, Peter again denied being a disciple: "I am not; I do not know the man."

About an hour later as Peter was walking about in the courtyard, the brother of Malchus, whose ear Peter had cut off, saw Peter. This man also accused Peter of being one of Our Lord's disciples. Peter, in a state of terror, began to curse and swear that he did not know Jesus. At that moment, the cock crowed.

At that same instant, Jesus was being led out across the courtyard. Turning, He looked with love and sadness upon Peter. Our Lord's look pierced Peter to his heart. He immediately recalled Our Lord's words: "Before the cock crows, you will deny Me three times."

Peter asks the Blessed Mother to forgive him.

Peter was overcome with grief. Despite the promise that he had made to Jesus that he would die rather than deny Him, he had denied Him. Cowardice had made him lie and curse. Peter left the courtyard and wept bitterly.

[There is a tradition that says that after Peter denied Jesus, every time he heard a rooster crow, he would weep bitterly. Peter's sorrow for denying Jesus was so deep, that his tears formed furrows in his cheeks.]

For the next forty-eight hours, Peter disappears from history. Where Peter went and what he did is not known. He did not go with John to Golgotha because he was ashamed to face the Blessed Mother. Yet, Peter's love for Our Lord was too strong and too deep for him to abandon Our Lord. Almost certainly Peter was somewhere nearby watching events unfold.

The Death of Judas

While the Temple guards were mistreating Jesus, Judas had been wandering the town. When Judas learned that Jesus had been condemned to death, he was filled with a terrible remorse. Yet, he did not run to Peter or one of the other Apostles to confess his sin. Rather, he ran to the Temple where the chief priests had gathered.

Judas approached the chief priests and frantically tore the moneybag containing the thirty pieces of silver from his waist. He held the bag out to them and demanded that they take it back. He admitted that he had sinned grievously by betraying an innocent man. The priests answered with contempt that it was not their business if he had the blood of an innocent man on his hands. They refused to even touch the moneybag. Filled with despair, Judas tore open the moneybag and threw the thirty silver coins down on the Temple floor. Then he fled the Temple to the outskirts of the town. Overcome with grief and believing that he had no hope for forgiveness, Judas hanged himself.

After Judas left, the chief priests gathered up the thirty silver pieces. However, because it was blood money, it was against Jewish law to put it in the Temple treasury. They used the money to buy Potter's Field as a cemetery for foreigners. However, the field was always known as "the Field of Blood."

Chapter Review — Fill in the blanks to complete the sentences below.

1. Though Peter was in disguise in Caiaphas' courtyard, he was recognized because _____.

2. Peter denied Our Lord _____ times.

3. What did Judas do with the thirty pieces of silver? _____

4. What did Judas do when he left the Temple? _____

Chapter 21

Jesus before the Roman Governor Pontius Pilate

Jesus before Herod

Jesus Is Taken to Pilate

In the morning, the Sanhedrin reassembled and again condemned Jesus to death. However, as Judea was a Roman province, the Jews lacked the authority to execute anyone. They needed to receive permission from the Roman governor before they could carry out a capital punishment. Therefore, they had to take Jesus before Pontius Pilate, the Roman governor.

The high priests and the Pharisees walked at the head of a long procession of people taking Jesus to see Pilate. At about eight in the morning, the procession reached Pilate's palace. The soldiers dragged Jesus before Pilate.

Pilate had long disliked the Jews and their religion. He especially detested the Sanhedrin and the Pharisees. Their treatment of Our Lord only increased Pilate's contempt for them. Pilate almost immediately saw the innocence of Jesus and the malevolence of His accusers. As a result, he quickly informed them that he was not going to condemn Jesus without proof.

In his most scornful voice, Pilate asked the Jewish leaders what charges they brought against Jesus. The Jews said that there were three charges. First, Jesus incited people to rebellion and violence. Secondly, He forbade people to pay their taxes to the Romans. Thirdly, Jesus declared that He was the Messiah, a King.

Pilate asked Jesus if He was a king. Jesus said that He was a king, but that His kingdom was not of this world. When Pilate heard Jesus' response to his questions, he told the Jews that he could find no fault with Jesus. At this announcement, the enemies of Jesus went wild! They cried out that Jesus was guilty of starting riots all over Judea. They claimed He caused riots from Galilee to Jerusalem.

Pilate Sends Jesus to Herod

When Pilate heard that Jesus was from Galilee, he had an idea. He asked if Jesus were a Galilean. When Jesus confirmed that He was from Galilee, Pilate ordered Jesus to be taken before Herod, the governor of Galilee. Pilate knew that Herod was in Jerusalem for the Passover Feast.

Pilate was very pleased with himself. He did not want to judge Jesus, and he knew that Herod was very interested in Our Lord. The Jews led Jesus to see Herod, whose palace was only a short distance away.

Having to take Jesus to Herod made Our Lord's enemies even angrier. They had hoped that Pilate would give them a swift decision. Now they had to see Herod. On the walk to Herod's palace, they vented their rage upon Our Lord.

Before the Jews left with Jesus, Pilate had sent a message to Herod that they were coming, so Herod was expecting them. The moment they entered his presence, the chief priests began to make accusations about Our Lord. However, Herod was in no hurry to render a decision about Jesus. In fact, Herod was very pleased and excited to meet Jesus. He knew a lot about Our Lord and had many questions. Herod also had heard that Jesus performed miracles, so Herod asked Jesus to perform a miracle.

However, Jesus refused to say a single word to Herod. Our Lord kept His eyes focused on the floor. Jesus refused to talk to Herod because of his adulterous marriage to his brother's wife, Herodias. Also, Herod had murdered John the Baptist.

Herod finally realized that Jesus would not speak to him, nor perform for him. Thus, Herod decided to mock Our Lord and call Him crazy. Herod and his soldiers made fun of Jesus and treated Him with contempt. Herod had Jesus dressed in a fine robe and sent back to Pilate.

By not condemning a man that Pilate had also chosen not to condemn, Herod was allowing Pilate to make the final decision. This was a good political move for Herod. He was returning the compliment that Pilate paid to him when Pilate allowed him to decide the fate of Our Lord. This act of courtesy on the part of both men caused them to reconcile with each other. Before this, Pilate and Herod had been enemies.

Jesus Appears Again before Pilate

Once again the Pharisees and the chief priests had their soldiers drag Jesus through the streets of Jerusalem to Pilate's palace. Our Lord's enemies were incredibly angry at having to return to Pilate who had already declared Jesus innocent a number of times.

By the time the mob dragging Jesus reached Pilate's palace it was late morning. During the day, the agents of the Sanhedrin had worked to stir the people up against Jesus. Thus, a very large crowd arrived at Pilate's palace.

During Our Lord's trial, Pilate had tried to release Him because he saw that Jesus was clearly innocent. However, Pilate was not a courageous man. He was just an average Roman official. Still, under normal conditions Pilate would provide good government; however, he feared two things. One was a riot. A year earlier during the Passover Feast, there had been a riot. As a result, he had stationed almost one thousand soldiers around his palace and the other government buildings.

To add to Pilate's problems, his wife Claudia had spoken with him at length about a dream that she had had the night before. The dream had filled her with terror. From her dream Claudia knew that Jesus was a good and holy man. Claudia begged Pilate not to harm Jesus. Claudia's words greatly troubled Pilate. Before he left her, Pilate promised not to condemn Jesus. [There is a tradition that says that Claudia became a Christian and a close friend of St. Paul.]

When the Jews brought Jesus before Pilate the second time, he called the chief priests and the people together. He told them that he had examined Jesus and not found Him guilty of any of the crimes of which He had been accused. Pilate also noted that Herod had also not found Him guilty. Therefore, Pilate said he would have Jesus whipped and released.

When the Pharisees heard Pilate's words they became enraged. They inflamed the people into a frenzy and called for Our Lord's death. Still, Pilate tried one last time to save Jesus.

Barabbas

There was a custom among the Jews that during Passover the governor could release a prisoner. Pilate, hoping to save Jesus, presented the Jews with a choice of prisoners. They could choose Jesus, or they could choose a man named Barabbas. Barabbas was a thief and a murderer. When offered the choice, the crowd yelled, "Barabbas!"

Again Pilate asked whom they wanted him to release. Again the crowd yelled, "Barabbas!" When Pilate asked what they wanted him to do with Jesus, the people shouted, "Crucify him!"

"What crime has he committed?" Pilate asked. Sadly, the crowd screamed even louder, "Crucify him!"

The crowd yelled, "Barabbas!"

The Prayer of the Blessed Mother

From the fringe of the crowd, the Blessed Mother witnessed this horrible scene. Mary knew that Jesus had to die in order to redeem the world. Yet Jesus was her Baby. She had carried him inside herself for nine months. As a young Boy, He had run to her when He was hungry or scared. Mary was filled with anguish and the desire to save her Son from the terrible torture and death He was about to suffer. Yet, like her Son, her will was in perfect obedience to the Will of God. Thus, in this terrible moment as Pilate wavered back and forth she prayed. "If possible let this cup pass, but not my will but Thine be done."

Chapter Review

Fill in the blanks to complete the sentences below.

1. _____ was the Roman governor of Judea before whom Christ was taken for judgment.

2. Why was King Herod anxious to meet Jesus? _____

_____

3. Jesus refused to speak to Herod because _____

and _____ .

4. How did Claudia, the Roman governor's wife, know that Jesus was innocent? _____

_____

5. The Jewish mob demanded that _____ be released instead of Jesus.

Chapter 22   The Scourging and the Crowning

The Crowning with Thorns

The Scourging at the Pillar

Pilate was still determined not to condemn Jesus to death. However, he was afraid the Jews in the mob might riot. Thus, in the hope of saving Jesus and satisfying the mob, Pilate ordered that Jesus be whipped.

Pilate's guards led Jesus to the place of scourging where six leather-clad men awaited Him. They stripped off the cloak that Herod had given Our Lord. Then the men tied His hands to an iron ring in a pillar. When Jesus was secured to the pillar, the six men beat Him with whips.

During the time that Our Lord was being scourged, Pilate tried to calm the crowd, which had been calling for Jesus to be crucified. Despite Pilate's efforts, the crowd continued to scream for Our Lord's death. They cried for His execution even if they had to die for it.

The Crowning with Thorns

After they scourged Him, the soldiers led Jesus from the pillar to the guardhouse. As He passed the high priests, they shouted, "Crucify Him!" In the guardhouse, the soldiers took turns mocking Our Lord. They covered Him in a purple garment. Then, they formed a crown out of thorns and pushed it into His head. Most of the thorns turned inward in order to pierce Our Lord's head. Once this terrible crown had been added to His agonies, the soldiers put a reed in His hands as if it were a royal scepter. They bowed down before Him saying, "Hail, King of the Jews!" Then they took the reed and struck Him with it, driving the thorns deeper into His head.

"Behold the Man"

The soldiers then escorted Jesus back to Pilate. Pilate, staring at the beaten and bloody body of Our Lord, was moved to pity. He thought

"Behold the man!"

that the people, if they saw the terrible torture inflicted upon Jesus, would also be moved to pity. Thus, Pilate decided to take Jesus out on a high balcony and show Him to the people.

Pilate ordered that a trumpet be sounded to quiet the mob. Then he had Jesus led out on the balcony. Pilate pointed to Jesus and said, "Behold the man!" However, the sight of Jesus did not fill His enemies with pity. His beaten body increased the fury of the high priests and their followers in the mob. Some in the mob, who on Palm Sunday had believed He was the Messiah, may have changed their minds at the sight of Our Lord. For these people, Jesus was not the kind of Messiah that they expected. Perhaps He was an imposter

who deserved to die. Thus, the mob continued to demand that Jesus be crucified.

Pilate was now totally uncertain what to do next. He went back inside his palace to question Our Lord once again. When Jesus refused to speak to him, Pilate reminded Jesus that he had the power to crucify Him or set Him free. Jesus replied that Pilate would have no authority unless it came from God.

Pilate returned to the balcony and once again said that he would release Jesus. The high priests and Pharisees then shouted out that if he released Jesus he was no friend of Caesar. This last statement made an impression on Pilate. The wrath of Tiberius Caesar, the vengeful ruler of the Roman

Jesus carries His cross.

Empire, was the second thing that Pilate feared.

Pilate called for a basin of water. In front of the screaming mob, he washed his hands saying, "I am innocent of the blood of this just man." In response, a dreadful cry came from the vast mob: "Let His blood be upon us and upon our children."

Jesus Takes Up His Cross

Thus, unable to stop the mob from demanding the death of Jesus, Pilate sentenced Him to death. The soldiers brought a heavy cross, which they placed upon Our Lord's shoulders. They tied a rope around Christ's waist so that they could drag Him through the streets. Then they led Him to Calvary, the place where criminals were executed.

Meanwhile, Pilate wrote an inscription for the cross: "Jesus of Nazareth, the King of the Jews." The chief priests objected to this notice. They wanted it changed, but Pilate refused. He angrily told them that what he had written would remain written!

As Jesus carried His cross through the streets of Jerusalem, He fell three times. After falling the third time, He was too weak to rise. The soldiers realized that unless someone carried the cross for Him, Jesus would die on the way to Calvary. At this moment, Simon the Cyrene passed by with his family. Simon was a muscular man who was coming in from working in the fields. The soldiers grabbed him and forced Him to help Jesus carry the cross. Though there is no record of any discussion between Simon and Jesus, tradition teaches that it was not long before the Holy Spirit touched his heart. Simon and his family would later become Catholics.

Veronica

About two hundred feet from where Simon began to help Jesus, the door of a beautiful house opened. From the house came a woman and her young daughter. This brave woman walked to the head of the procession of people. She pushed her way through the crowd and fell on her knees before Jesus. She carried a long veil, which she presented to Jesus and asked if she could wipe His battered face. Jesus took the veil, wiped His bleeding face, and returned it to her with His thanks.

When the woman returned home, she placed the veil on her kitchen table and almost passed out. On the woolen veil Our Lord had left a perfect likeness of His face. It is from this incident that the Church has given this courageous woman the name "Veronica," from the Latin *vera icon*, which means "true image."

Jesus Speaks to the Women of Jerusalem

Shortly after Veronica's act of kindness, Jesus turned to the crowd that followed him. In the crowd were many women. Most of the women were young women or young mothers with small children. Our Lord's terrible suffering touched these women who were crying. Turning to them, Jesus tried to console them. Despite His own incredible agony, He spoke to them kindly. He told them not to weep for Him, but for themselves and their children.

Veronica wipes the face of Jesus.

Chapter Review

Fill in the blanks to complete the sentences below.

1. What were the two things that Pontius Pilate feared? _____ _____

2. In the hopes of saving Jesus' life, Pilate ordered that He _____; afterwards, the Roman soldiers mocked Jesus and _____.

3. _____ was a muscular man whom the Roman soldiers grabbed and forced to help Jesus carry His cross.

4. The name "Veronica," comes from the Latin words *vera icon*, which means _____.

5. Our Lord left a perfect impression of His face on Veronica's _____.

Chapter 23 — The Death of Our Lord

Jesus Is Nailed to the Cross

About fifteen minutes before noon, Jesus arrived at the spot on Calvary where He was to be crucified. It was called Golgotha, the Place of the Skull. He sank to the ground under the terrible weight of the cross. The soldiers tried to give Our Lord some wine mixed with a drug called myrrh that would deaden His senses. However, Jesus would not drink it. He was determined to endure the full agony of His crucifixion for our sins. The executioners then dug holes for three crosses, as Jesus was to be crucified along with two thieves.

The executioners pulled off the garment that Our Lord was wearing, leaving Him in only His undergarments. Then they nailed His hands and feet to the cross. When Jesus had been nailed to the cross, the commander of the Roman soldiers ordered that Pilate's plaque be nailed to the top of the cross. On each side of Him, they crucified one of the thieves. Then the executioners divided Our Lord's clothes and threw dice to see who would get which piece of clothing.

Jesus Hangs on the Cross

As Jesus hung suffering on the cross, the Pharisees sauntered past and

Jesus hangs upon the cross.

mocked Him. They scornfully yelled up at Him that He said that He could destroy the Temple and rebuild it in three days, so if He was the Son of God, He should come down from the cross. They said if He did that, then they would believe in Him. The Roman soldiers also called mockingly up to Him. Jesus' only response was a prayer of forgiveness to His Holy Father:

"Father, forgive them, for they know not what they do."

One of the thieves, named Gesmas, hanging beside Our Lord also began to insult Him. Gesmas mocked, "Aren't you the Messiah? Save yourself and us!" However, Jesus' prayer of forgiveness had touched the heart of the other thief, who was named Dismas. In a loud clear voice he exclaimed to Gesmas, "How can you insult Him when He prays for you? He has suffered all these tortures in silence. He truly is the Son of God! We are criminals and are justly punished, but this Man is innocent."

Then Dismas turned to Jesus. He confessed his sins to Jesus and asked for forgiveness. Jesus forgave his sins and promised: "This day you shall be with Me in Paradise."

[There is a tradition that as a child, Dismas had been cured of leprosy by Jesus and Mary. Leonardo da Vinci's magnificent painting *The Virgin of the Rocks* is based upon this tradition. The tradition says that as he hung upon the cross, Dismas remembered the act of kindness which Jesus and His mother had done for him.]

The Sorrowful Mother

The Blessed Mother, the Blessed Mother's sister-in-law Mary, Mary Magdalene, and St. John stood at the foot of the cross gazing up at Our Lord. Looking down, His vision dimming, Jesus spoke to them. Looking at John, He said to His Blessed Mother, "Woman, behold thy son." Then to John, he said, "Behold thy mother." From that moment, John considered Mary to be his mother. He would treat her as his mother and care for her until her death. So overcome was Our Lady at these words that she nearly fainted. She had to be carried a short distance from the cross by the other holy women.

Our Lord's Death

At the time that the soldiers nailed Jesus to the cross, darkness had begun to cover Calvary. With all the shouting and excitement, people had not immediately noticed the change. As the darkness grew, so did the terror in the hearts of the people. Before long, the mob became silent. Even the Pharisees in their fear no longer shouted at Jesus.

Around the cross, all was still. About three o'clock, Jesus broke the silence when He cried out in a loud voice, "My God, My God, why have You forsaken Me?" At these words, Mary rushed back to the foot of the cross.

Then Jesus, His throat parched with dryness, said, "I thirst." A soldier dipped a sponge in a bowl of cheap wine, put the sponge on the end of a reed, and lifted it to Our Lord's lips. When Jesus had tasted the wine, He said, "It is finished." Then He cried out in a loud clear voice, "Father, into Your hands I commend My spirit." He bowed His head and died.

At the moment of Our Lord's death, the Earth trembled. The rock of Calvary split apart. Graves were opened, and the dead arose. The huge eighty-two by twenty-four foot curtain hanging in the Temple was torn in two from top to bottom. Abenadar, the centurion in command of the Roman soldiers, underwent a conversion experience. He cried out in a loud voice, "Truly this Man was the Son of God!" *Many of his men, hearing his words, were also converted.*

Now a follower of Christ, Abenadar could no longer serve the Roman Empire. He gave his horse and his lance to Longinus, his next-in-command. Abenadar left Calvary and went to seek out Christ's disciples.

Abenadar's public profession of faith stirred many who also came to believe in

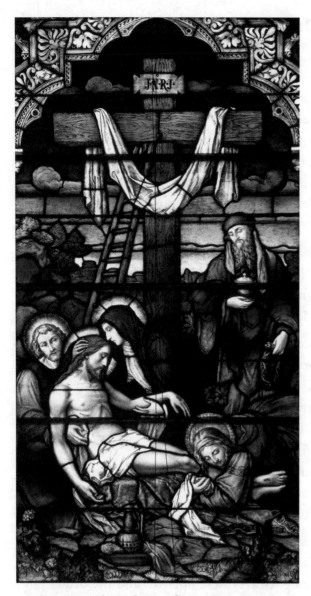

Jesus is taken down from the cross.

the Sabbath dawned. (Crucifixion is an agonizingly slow method of death. The person slowly suffocates to death. To breathe, a man must push up with his legs. Once the legs are broken it is no longer possible to breathe, and death occurs quickly.) Pilate readily agreed to break the legs of the condemned men and sent soldiers to Calvary to carry out his order.

Pilate's soldiers broke the legs of Dismas and Gesmas; however, when they came to Jesus, He was already dead. Rather than break His legs, Longinus pierced Christ's side with his lance. At once, blood and water poured from Our Lord's side.

[A tradition teaches that the blood and water from Christ's side flowed over Longinus. It had the effect of Baptism, and grace immediately entered his soul. He jumped off his horse and declared that Jesus was God.]

In the evening, Nicodemus and Joseph of Arimathea, members of the Sanhedrin, but also secret followers of Jesus, asked Pilate for the body of Jesus. They wanted to at least give Jesus a decent burial. Pilate agreed to give them the body. Joseph and Nicodemus had decided to bury Our Lord in a new tomb that Joseph had made at the end of his garden, not far from Calvary.

Joseph and Nicodemus came and took Our Lord's body from Calvary. First, they had the sacred body washed. Then, they had the body embalmed with precious perfumes. Finally, they wrapped His body in a white linen shroud and laid it in the tomb. They rolled a large stone across the entrance to the tomb and went home.

The Murderers Meet

Meanwhile, the men who had murdered Our Lord were very nervous. Late on Friday night, Caiaphas, the Pharisees, and the leaders

Our Lord. The people returned to Jerusalem weeping and beating their chests, fearing that a great sin had been committed. Some tore their clothes and put dust on their heads. From a distance, Mary, St. John, and their friends watched as the others departed.

Jesus Is Buried

Our Lord and the two thieves had been crucified on the eve of the Jewish Sabbath. The members of the Sanhedrin went to Pilate to ask him that the legs of the three men be broken in order that they might die before of the Sanhedrin held a meeting. They must have been affected by what had happened in the Temple that afternoon. The darkness and the earthquake had affected all of Jerusalem. They were also uneasy about the things that Jesus had said while He was alive: "After three days, I will rise again." They were afraid that Our Lord's disciples would steal His body and claim that He had risen. In fact, Our Lord's body was in a tomb now under the control of Christ's followers. The murderers argued all night and into the morning before they went to see Pilate.

 At Pilate's house, the Jewish leaders demanded that Pilate seal the tomb and place a guard on it. Pilate, sick of these Jews, reluctantly agreed. The Sanhedrin went with a squad of Roman soldiers that was ordered to seal and guard the tomb.

(Though there is no historical evidence, it seems logical that before sealing the tomb the members of the Sanhedrin would have looked inside to verify that Jesus was in fact still there. To have sealed an empty tomb would be illogical. To seal the tomb without checking for Our Lord's body also flies in the face of human nature. These men were paranoid that the body might be stolen. They would have looked inside the tomb.)

Chapter Review — Fill in the blanks to complete the sentences below.

1. The spot on Calvary where Jesus was crucified is called

   _____.

2. As He hung on the cross, Jesus forgave the sins of _____.

3. _____ were Our Lord's last

   words before He died.

4. At Our Lord's death, the huge eighty-two by twenty-four foot curtain hanging in

   the Temple _____.

5. After Jesus' death, _____ and

   _____, members of the Sanhedrin,

   but also secret followers of Jesus, asked Pilate for Our Lord's body.

6. Fearing that the disciples would steal Christ's body,

   _____ demanded that Pilate seal the tomb and place a

   guard on it.

Chapter 24

The Resurrection

The Resurrection

The Resurrection

For two days, Jesus' body had lain in the tomb. As the sun was rising on Sunday morning of the third day, a massive earthquake shocked the sixteen Roman guards on duty! Suddenly, an angel appeared and rolled back the huge stone slab that covered the mouth of Our Lord's tomb. From the tomb, they saw what they did not imagine to be possible: Jesus coming out of the tomb! His face shone like the sun. In utter terror, these hardened Roman warriors, these men who had conquered the known world, threw themselves to the ground. When at last they had control of themselves, they fled to Jerusalem to inform Pilate what had happened.

The Empty Tomb

A short time after the soldiers departed, Mary Magdalene, Mary the mother of James, and Mary, the Blessed Mother's sister-in-law, came to the tomb. They intended to finish washing and to anoint Our Lord's body with spices. They had not been able to complete their work the previous Friday with the arrival of the Sabbath. As they walked, they wondered who would roll away the huge stone that covered the tomb entrance. However, when they arrived at the tomb, they saw that the stone was already rolled back. Astonished, they entered the tomb.

Inside the tomb, the three women saw the shroud in which Our Lord had been wrapped. They also saw a young man (an angel) sitting on the right side of the tomb. The sight of the young man filled them with fear, but he told them not to be afraid. The young man said that he knew that they were looking for Jesus, but that He had risen. The angel told them to go and tell Peter and the other Apostles.

Mary Magdalene immediately ran to the house where the Apostles were staying. Peter and John opened the door for her. She told them that someone had taken Our Lord's body, and she did not know where they had placed Him. Then she turned and sprinted back to the tomb. Peter and John chased after her.

John was much younger and faster than Peter, so he arrived at the tomb before his older friend. Yet, Peter was the head of the Apostles, so John waited until Peter arrived. Peter entered the tomb followed by John. Inside, they found only Our Lord's burial shroud. Peter took the shroud and hid it under his cloak. Then the two men hurried back to tell the other Apostles the wonderful news.

Jesus Appears to His Blessed Mother

Catholic tradition has always maintained that the first person Jesus appeared to after His Resurrection was His Blessed Mother. Logically, Jesus would appear to His own mother who had shared His life, His sorrows, and His joys, at this His moment of triumph. Not to appear to her would have been cruel for any son, and impossible for Jesus.

The strongest evidence in support of the Catholic tradition is that Mary did not go with the other three women to the tomb to anoint Jesus' body. Mary, who loved Him more than any other person had ever or will ever love Him, did not accompany the other

Jesus Appears to His Blessed Mother

thought the man was the gardener since he carried a spade and wore a wide brimmed hat.[1] Then the man asked for whom she was looking. At this question, Mary Magdalene asked the man if he had taken Our Lord's body and where it was. Then Jesus said to her, "Mary."

Mary Magdalene instantly recognized Jesus when He said her name and threw herself on her knees before Him. (For some reason, His followers did not always immediately recognize Jesus in His glorified body.) Mary stretched out her hands to embrace Him; however, He stepped back from her. He told her not to touch Him. Rather, she should tell His Apostles that He was going to Galilee and that they would see Him there.

Then Jesus said to her, "Mary."

three women when they went to the tomb. The only reasonable explanation for her not to go to the tomb is that she *knew* that Jesus had left it. She knew because her Son had already visited her.

Jesus Appears to Mary Magdalene

Peter and John had barely left the tomb to spread the joyous news when Mary Magdalene arrived back at the tomb. Crying, filled with sorrow, she longed to find Our Lord's body. As she looked around, she noticed a tall man standing in the garden about ten yards away from her partly hidden behind a palm tree.

Mary Magdalene was startled when the man kindly asked why she was crying. Mary

The Chief Priests and Pharisees Learn of the Resurrection

In the meantime, some of the soldiers who had been guarding Our Lord's tomb arrived back in Jerusalem with the news of the Resurrection. They went to the chief priests and told them what had happened. Caiaphas quickly assembled the Sanhedrin, and the members discussed how they should proceed. They agreed that they needed to bribe the tomb guards to keep them from spreading the news of the Resurrection. The chief priest told the guards to say that Jesus' disciples came during the night and stole the body while they were sleeping. Caiaphas assured the soldiers that, if Pilate learned of these events, he would give him a large bribe as well to keep them out of trouble.

[1] According to the visions of Anne Catherine Emmerich

It is clear that Caiaphas and the other leaders believed the guards' story. They simply refused to believe that Jesus was the Son of God as He had claimed. The Pharisees also realized that they could not allow the guards to spread their story. The Jewish people could not hear the news that Jesus had risen from the dead. Plainly, His Resurrection proved beyond doubt that He was the Son of God. All their work to discredit Him would be in vain. Thus, the chief priests gave a huge bribe to the Roman soldiers. They told the soldiers to say, "His disciples came by night and stole him while we were sleeping." [This story is purely ridiculous on its face. St. Augustine said it best: "How is this? Do you call upon witnesses who were asleep?"]

The standard detachment of Roman soldiers assigned to guard duty typically consisted of sixteen men. Four were on watch at all times. Sleeping on watch was a crime punishable by death. Moreover, Pilate's residence was only six hundred yards from Our Lord's tomb. Since it was a capital offense for a soldier to sleep on duty, the chief priests had to promise to protect the soldiers by bribing Pilate.

The tomb guards took the bribe and told the tale as they had been instructed. The false story spread among the Jewish people. That anyone then or now could believe such a story is beyond rationality. Rather, for those

The supper at Emmaus

who have chosen not to believe, this provides an excuse for that disbelief. There are none so deaf as those who will not hear.

Jesus on the Road to Emmaus

On Sunday evening, two of Our Lord's disciples were walking from Jerusalem to Emmaus. As they strolled, they discussed the events of the past few days. Jesus strode up beside them, but for some reason they did not recognize Him. Jesus asked the two men what they were talking about. One of the men, named Cleopas, asked Jesus if He were a visitor to Jerusalem. Otherwise, how did He not know of the events of the past few days?

Cleopas and his companion then told Our Lord of the events that had recently transpired in Jerusalem. They explained that they had come to believe that Jesus was the Messiah, but that He had been handed over to the chief priests. Then Pilate had ordered that He be crucified. That was three days ago. Now some of Christ's followers were saying that He had risen from the dead.

When the two finished speaking, Jesus explained to them what the Scriptures had said about Him. He explained how it had been necessary for Our Lord to suffer and die as He had.

As they approached Emmaus, Jesus acted as if He intended to continue on past the town. However, Cleopas urged Him to stay with them in Emmaus, as it was nearly evening and growing dark. So He agreed to have dinner with them.

Sitting at the table, Our Lord took bread, blessed it, then broke it and gave it to them. At once their eyes were opened and they recognized Him. However, Jesus immediately vanished from their sight.

Jesus Appears but His Apostles Doubt

After Jesus had vanished, Cleopas and his friend rushed to Jerusalem to tell the eleven Apostles that they had seen Our Lord. The Apostles were very excited because Peter and Mary Magdalene had earlier told them that they had both seen Jesus. Cleopas told the Apostles how they had met Jesus on the road to Emmaus and how they had come to

know it was He when He offered up the Holy Eucharist.

While everyone was speaking, Jesus suddenly appeared in the middle of the room. Everyone was startled and afraid. They thought that they were seeing a ghost. Yet Jesus calmed them. He said, "Peace be with you." Then, to prove that He was no spirit, He told them to touch His hands and His feet. He was no ghost, but flesh and blood as they were.

When Our Lord's followers still doubted, He asked them if they had anything to eat. They gave Him a piece of baked fish. He took it and ate it.

Jesus Institutes the Sacrament of Confession

At last the Apostles believed that it was indeed Jesus in their midst. Then Jesus told His Apostles that as the Father had sent Him, He was now sending them forth. In fact, this commission confirmed the eleven as *Apostles*, a word that means "those sent." He commanded them to go forth and make disciples of all nations. They were to baptize in the name of the Father, the Son, and the Holy Spirit. They were to teach all nations to follow God's laws.

Moreover, just as God breathed on Adam to give him life, Our Lord breathed on the Apostles to give them new spiritual life. As He breathed on them, He said, "Receive the Holy Spirit. Whose sins you forgive are forgiven them, and whose sins you retain are retained." By this act, Jesus gave the Apostles and their successors the power to forgive sins.

In these two vital commissions, to teach all nations and to forgive sins, which Jesus gave to the Apostles, we have undeniable proof of the divine nature of the Catholic Church and the power of the Catholic priesthood. The

Apostles would die, but the Catholic Church will live forever. Thus, the power Christ gave to the Apostles was not only given to them, but also to their successors, the priests and bishops of the Catholic Church.

From the very beginning, Catholic priests and bishops have always claimed the power and authority to forgive sins. It is not an invention of the thirteenth century as some historians would like us to believe. The power to forgive sins is exercised through the Sacrament of Penance (Reconciliation), a Sacrament instituted by Jesus when He appeared to His Apostles after He rose from the dead.

Chapter Review   Fill in the blanks to complete the sentences below.

1. _____ were the first three people to visit the empty tomb on Easter morning.

2. _____ were the first two Apostles to visit the empty tomb.

3. Catholic tradition has always maintained that the first person Jesus appeared to after His resurrection was _____.

4. What evidence supports this tradition?_____

_____

5. When Mary Magdalene first saw the Risen Christ she mistook Him for_____

_____.

6. Why is the story told by the Roman soldiers guarding Jesus' tomb unbelievable?

_____

_____

7. While walking to _____, Jesus met two of His disciples who failed to recognize Him.

8. When and how did Jesus institute the Sacrament of Reconciliation (Penance)?

_____

_____

Chapter 25

"Simon, Do You Love Me More Than These?"

Peter replied, "Lord, You know that I love You."

Doubting Thomas

When Jesus appeared to the Apostles, Thomas had not been with them. When Thomas returned from his errand, the other Apostles told him what had happened. While Thomas did not think that they were lying,

Thomas was a man who wanted to see things for himself. He trusted his friends but wanted to verify what they said. Thus, Thomas told the others that unless he could see the mark of the nails in Our Lord's hands and feet, and touch the wound in Our Lord's side, he would not believe.

A week later, the Apostles were again locked in their room. This time, Thomas was with them. Suddenly, Jesus appeared in their midst. "Peace be with you," He said.

Turning to Thomas, Our Lord told him to put his finger into Our Lord's side and to look at the wounds in His hands and feet. Falling to his knees in shame, Thomas cried out, "My Lord and my God!" Then, not unkindly, Jesus said to Thomas, "Because you have seen Me, you believe. Blessed are they that have not seen and have believed."

(In one of history's most interesting ironies, St. Thomas in his missionary journey was sent to India. The people of India did not believe in spiritual things. They would

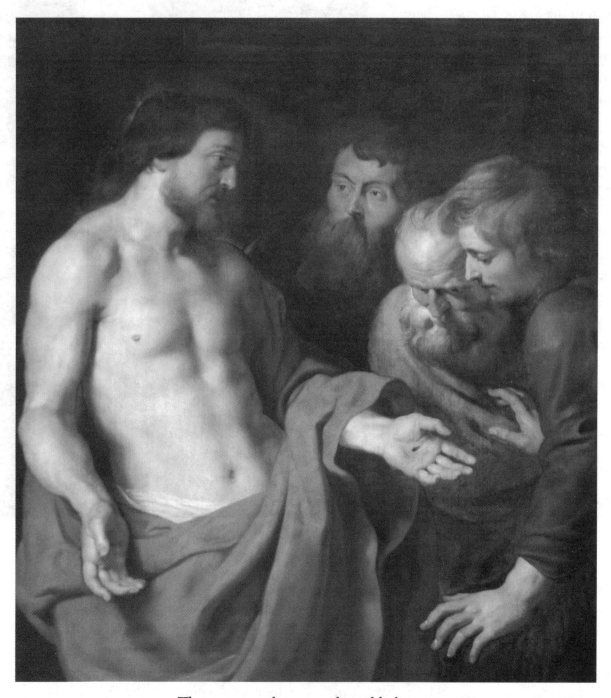

Thomas sees the wounds and believes.

only believe in those things that they could see and touch. Thus, St. Thomas was the perfect Apostle to evangelize them.)

Jesus Reaffirms Peter as the First Pope

After appearing to Thomas and the others, Jesus ordered them to go to the Sea of Tiberias. There, Jesus appeared to them for a third time. As the Apostles were fishing, Jesus again performed a miracle, causing their nets to fill with fish.

When the Apostles hauled the fish to shore, Our Lord greeted them. They had a breakfast of bread and fish. When they had finished eating, Jesus addressed Peter. "Simon, do you love Me more than these?" Peter answered, "Yes, Lord, You know I love You." Jesus said, "Feed My lambs."

A second time Jesus asked if Peter loved Him. A second time Peter said that he did. Jesus told Peter to "tend My sheep."

For a third time, Jesus asked Peter if he loved Him. Now Peter had become upset that Jesus had asked him the question three times. Peter replied, "Lord, You know everything. You know that I love You." Jesus said, "Feed My sheep."

Our Lord asked Peter if he loved Him three times because Peter had denied Him three times. Peter's three-fold confession counteracts his three denials on the night of Our Lord's arrest. The *lambs* and the *sheep* are the faithful and the priests and bishops of the Church. When the

The Ascension

First Vatican Council officially declared the Doctrine of Papal Infallibility, it cited John 21:15-17 as part of the basis for that doctrine. The Vatican Council said that Jesus gave Peter the jurisdiction of supreme shepherd and ruler over the entire flock. This jurisdiction continues in the popes, the legitimate successors of St. Peter.

The Promise of the Holy Spirit

After He made Peter the head of His Church, Our Lord appeared to the Apostles again. On these occasions, He spoke to them about the future of the Church and their roles in it. He also spoke about their future missionary efforts.

Forty days after His Resurrection, Jesus appeared to His Apostles for the final time on Mount Olivet. He told them not to leave Jerusalem but to wait there awhile. Jesus promised them that in a few days they would receive the Holy Spirit. Once they had received the Holy Spirit, they should go forth and preach the Gospel all over the world. Our Lord's promise was fulfilled on Pentecost when the Holy Spirit appeared as tongues of fire and filled the Apostles with special graces.

The Ascension

After Our Lord had promised His Apostles the power of the Holy Spirit, He began to ascend into Heaven. Soon, He ascended through a cloud and they could no longer see Him. While they were still looking up, two angels dressed in shining white robes appeared above them. The two angels said that Jesus had been taken up into Heaven, but He would one day return again in the same way. Then the Apostles returned to Jerusalem to await the coming of the Holy Spirit.

The Election of Matthias

After the Ascension, the Apostles stayed in Jerusalem. They remained in the upper room where they had stayed since the Resurrection. There, with Mary and about 120 of the other disciples, they dedicated themselves to prayer.

After a few days, Peter, as head of the Church, stood up and said that the time had come to replace Judas. (Judas needed to be replaced in order that the Catholic Church, the new Israel, would continue to have twelve Apostles, who corresponded to the twelve tribes of Israel.) Two men were proposed to replace the traitor. The Apostles prayed for guidance and chose Matthias.

Chapter Review — Fill in the blanks to complete the sentences below.

1. Why did Our Lord ask Peter if he loved Him three times?_____

_____

2. Who are the lambs and the sheep that Jesus told Peter to feed and tend?

_____

3. _____ replaced Judas as the twelfth Apostle.

Chapter 26

Pentecost

Pentecost

The Descent of the Holy Spirit

Ten days after Our Lord ascended into Heaven was the Jewish Feast of Pentecost. The Apostles had all gathered together in their upper room. Suddenly, they heard a noise like a hurricane blowing. The sound of a rushing wind filled the entire house. At the same time, tongues of fire came to rest on the head of each Apostle.

Immediately, the Apostles were all filled with the Holy Spirit. The Holy Spirit imparted special graces to the Apostles. They were imbued with great courage. No longer afraid of the Jews, they boldly left the upper room, determined to preach the Gospel.

Peter Speaks to the Crowd

Jews from many distant lands had traveled to Jerusalem to celebrate the great Feast of Pentecost. Also, many Jews had remained in Jerusalem following the Passover festival. When the people heard the incredible noise coming from the house where the Apostles were, they came to investigate. When they arrived at the house, they heard the Apostles preaching the Gospel. Yet, each listener heard the Apostles speaking perfectly in his own native language! The Apostles were no longer fearful or confused. The Holy Spirit had conferred upon the Apostles many gifts, not the least important of which was the virtue of fortitude.

The people in the huge crowd were shocked and confused. How was it possible that a group of Galileans were speaking, yet the listeners heard the words in their own language? Amazed and confused, the people kept asking, "What does this mean?" Some listeners tried to dismiss this miracle by claiming the Apostles were drunk. However,

Peter stood up and said that the Apostles were not drunk. Rather, it was the fulfillment of a prophecy.

Then Peter went on to speak about Jesus. Peter spoke of how Jesus had worked miracles and proved that He was the Son of God. Yet, evil men had crucified and killed Him. However, He had risen from the dead and was now in Heaven sitting at the right hand of God the Father. He had sent the Holy Spirit upon the Apostles. That was the miracle that the crowd was now witnessing. Peter concluded by telling them that Jesus whom they crucified was the Messiah.

Peter's words touched the people in the crowd, who were deeply troubled. Moreover, they could not deny the miracle by which the Apostles spoke to each person in their native

Peter told the crippled man to arise and walk in the name of Jesus.

tongue. Thus, the people asked Peter what they needed to do. Peter told them that they needed to repent and be baptized in the name of Jesus Christ. The Holy Spirit touched the minds and hearts of three thousand people, who were baptized that day. On this Pentecost, the Catholic Church was born. When the converted pilgrims returned to their homes in various lands, the worldwide expansion of the Catholic Church had begun.

(The symbolism between the Jewish Pentecost and the Catholic Pentecost is significant. The Jewish Pentecost was a harvest feast. During a harvest feast, the Holy Spirit made a rich harvest of converts. The Catholic Pentecost thus became a spiritual harvest, a harvest not of fruits and vegetables, but of souls.)

Peter preaches in the Temple.

Peter and John Cure a Crippled Beggar

A few days after Pentecost, Peter and John went to the Temple to pray. Every day, a man who had been crippled since his birth was placed in front of the Temple by his friends. Each day, he would beg for alms from the people entering the Temple.

When the crippled beggar saw Peter and John about to go into the Temple, he asked them for money. Peter told the man that he had no money. However, what Peter had was the power to cure the man. Peter took the man by his hand, pulled him up, and told him in the name of Jesus to arise and walk. Instantly, the man jumped up and began to praise God. Walking and jumping, he entered the Temple with Peter and John.

When the crowd of people in the Temple saw the man, whom they all knew as the crippled beggar, they were astonished. Peter, seeing their amazed faces, spoke to the people. Peter told them that it was through the power of Jesus Christ that the crippled beggar had been cured. Peter's speech was so powerful that five thousand people became Christians and were baptized right there.

Peter and John before the Sanhedrin

While Peter and John were still preaching to the people in the Temple, some priests and Temple guards arrived. Enraged to find the two Apostles openly preaching about Jesus, the priests ordered the guards to arrest them. The guards threw Peter and John into prison.

At this point, the Sanhedrin could not ignore the massive number of conversions to the Faith. They had to take action. The next day, the Sanhedrin assembled. Soldiers ushered Peter and John into the council hall. There, Caiaphas questioned them about their cure of the crippled man. Peter said that the cripple had been cured by the power and in the name of Jesus of Nazareth, whom they crucified. Peter also told them that Jesus had risen from the dead.

When Peter had finished speaking, the members of the Sanhedrin ordered them to leave the room. Then the members of the Sanhedrin conferred among themselves. They realized that everyone in Jerusalem knew that a miracle had been done. Everyone had seen the crippled man. He had begged outside the Temple for decades. The news of his cure had spread through Jerusalem like wildfire. Even the Sanhedrin could not deny it.

The Sanhedrin recalled Peter and John. They told the two Apostles not to speak or to teach in Jesus' name any longer. Peter, who had fled in fear on Good Friday morning, now boldly defied the entire Sanhedrin. Peter and John told them that they had to obey God. They had to speak about what they had seen and heard.

The Sanhedrin could do no more than threaten the Apostles and release them. The news of the cure was too widespread. It could not be covered up.

Chapter Review

Fill in the blanks to complete the sentences below.

1. The Holy Spirit descended upon the Apostles as _____ on the Feast of _____.

2. Why were the people in the crowd amazed when the Apostles spoke to them after the Holy Spirit descended upon them? _____

3. A few days after Pentecost, in front of the Temple, _____ _____ healed a man who had been crippled since his birth.

4. _____ told Peter and John to stop preaching.

Chapter 27

The Church Is Persecuted

St. Stephen is stoned to death.

Ananias and Sapphira Lie to the Apostles

Among the recent converts to the Faith were a man named Ananias and his wife Sapphira. The couple sold a piece of property that belonged to them and, though they promised to give all the proceeds of the sale to the Apostles, they kept some of the money for themselves. When Ananias gave the money to Peter, he pretended that he had given Peter all the money from the sale.

Peter was not fooled. He confronted Ananias. Peter told him that the property was Ananias' and that the money from the sale was his as well. However, he should not have lied and said that he had given away all the money. He had not simply lied to Peter; he had lied to God!

Peter had barely finished speaking when Ananias fell dead at Peter's feet. Three hours later, Sapphira came to see Peter. She did not know what had happened to her husband. Peter asked her about the sale of the land. She repeated her husband's lie, and then she too fell dead at Peter's feet.

The Apostles Are Persecuted

The Apostles continued to perform miracles and to preach the Gospel. People from all over Judea brought their sick friends and relatives to Jerusalem to be cured by the Apostles. Of all the Apostles, Peter was the most revered. So great was the power God gave to him, that as he walked down the street, people were cured when his shadow passed over them!

Of course, the growth of the Church and the esteem the people placed on Peter filled the High Priest and his followers with jealousy. Once again, they arrested Peter and John, and threw them into prison. However, during the night, an angel opened the doors of the prison and set the Apostles free.

The next morning, the jailors went to fetch the Apostles and bring them before the High Priest. Though the prison doors were locked, the Apostles were gone. The guards reported that they did not know where the Apostles were. As they were making their report to the confused council members, another guard came into the room and told

them that Peter and John were in the Temple teaching!

The captain of the Temple guard left with some soldiers. They brought Peter and John back to the Sanhedrin, but treated the Apostles very gently because the soldiers feared that the crowd would stone them if they mistreated the two men. Once again, the High Priest admonished Peter and John for teaching in public. Once again Peter and John defied the Sanhedrin and said that they were going to do God's Will.

Peter also told the Sanhedrin that Jesus, whom they had crucified, was the Messiah. He told them that Jesus had risen from the dead. When the members of the council heard Peter's words, they were furious. They began to think how they could kill Peter and John.

Peter and John were ordered to wait outside while a respected member of the Sanhedrin rose to speak. He warned the others not to act hastily. If Peter and John were doing God's work, then the Sanhedrin could not destroy it. His words persuaded the other members not to kill the two Apostles. Instead, they had Peter and John whipped. The council ordered them never to preach again and then released them.

The two Apostles left the council hall rejoicing. They were filled with joy at having the chance to suffer for Our Lord. (For Peter, being scourged may actually have been one of the happiest moments of his entire life because it meant that he had been found worthy to suffer for Jesus.) Of course, Peter and John ignored the Sanhedrin. They continued to preach about Jesus in the Temple, in people's homes, and anywhere else that people would listen to them.

The Martyrdom of St. Stephen

Stephen: The First Martyr

As the number of Christians increased, a dispute arose regarding the way in which food and money was distributed. When the Apostles learned of this problem, they realized that they could not take time from preaching to deal with these matters. Thus, they told the people to choose seven men, who were both honest and wise, whom the Apostles would place in charge of these matters. The people liked this plan and chose seven holy men whom they presented to the Apostles. The Apostles consecrated these men as deacons. They would take care of the temporal needs of the Church.

Among the seven deacons was a young man named Stephen. Stephen was very blessed by God and performed many miracles for the people. Stephen was also a gifted and forceful speaker.

Though the Jews, especially the Pharisees, did not like him, they could not refute his wisdom. However, his outspoken preaching about Jesus caused the Pharisees to want to silence him permanently.

As a result, the Pharisees bribed men to lie about Stephen. These false witnesses claimed that Stephen had spoken against Moses and blasphemed against God. These lies stirred up the people against Stephen. Stephen was seized and taken before the Sanhedrin where he was put on trial for his life. As he stood before the council, the members thought that they were looking at an angel.

Caiaphas stood up and asked Stephen if the charges against him were true. Rather than simply saying yes or no, Stephen responded by reviewing the history of the Jewish people. He showed how Judaism was the precursor of Catholicism. Stephen summed up by asking which of the prophets did the Jews not persecute? He concluded by telling the Sanhedrin that they had killed the Messiah.

When Stephen paused in his speech, the council members shook with rage. Yet Stephen had not finished speaking. He lifted up his eyes to Heaven and cried out, "Look, I see Heaven opened and the Son of Man standing at the right hand of God." Hearing these last words, the Council members all gave a loud cry and covered their ears. They screamed that he had blasphemed. In their fury they all rushed at Stephen. They dragged him out of the city and stoned him. [Stoning was the punishment for blasphemy. It also appears that the prohibition against the Jews killing anyone without the permission of the Romans had been suspended at this point in history, a suspension of which the Sanhedrin quickly took advantage.]

As they were stoning him, Stephen called out, "Lord Jesus, receive my spirit." Then in imitation of Our Blessed Lord, he knelt down and cried out, "Lord, do not hold this sin against them." With those words, he died.

Watching the stoning of Stephen with great approval was a young Jewish man named Saul, whose name in Greek was Paul. Saul had held the cloaks of those who had stoned Stephen so that they could more effectively throw their rocks. Those who witnessed the death of Stephen laid their cloaks at the feet of Saul.

As a devout Jew, Saul was certainly unmoved at the death of a blasphemer. However, the time would come when God would personally call upon Saul. Saul would undergo a conversion, and the world would never be the same.

Chapter Review

Fill in the blanks to complete the sentences below.

1. God struck _____ and _____ dead for lying to the Apostles about money they had donated.

2. _____ was the most revered of all the Apostles. People were cured when his shadow passed over them.

3. The Apostles consecrated seven men as _____ to care for the temporal needs of the Church.

4. _____ was the first martyr.

Chapter 28   The Conversion of Saul

"Saul, Saul! Why do you persecute Me?"

The Sacrament of Confirmation

Stephen's death marked the start of a terrible persecution of the Church in Jerusalem. Of all those persecuting the Church, none were more dedicated to its destruction than Saul. Saul went from house to house dragging out Christian men and women and throwing them into prison. Though the Apostles stayed in and around Jerusalem for about twelve more years, as the city became unsafe, members of the early Church scattered into the surrounding areas of Judea, Samaria, and Syria.

Among those who fled Jerusalem was Philip, one of the seven deacons. Philip left Jerusalem for Samaria where he preached the Gospel and performed many miracles. His preaching and miracles caused many people to be baptized and convert to the True Faith.

When the Apostles in Jerusalem heard of the good work that Philip had done in Samaria, they sent Peter and John to Samaria. In Samaria, Peter and John confirmed the men and women whom Philip had baptized.

The Baptism of the Ethiopian

After Philip had been in Samaria for a time, an angel appeared to him. The angel told Philip to travel down a certain road that led to Gaza. Philip did as the angel commanded.

On the road, Philip met an Ethiopian man sitting in his chariot, reading Isaiah the prophet. The man was the treasurer for the Queen of Ethiopia. The Ethiopian had been in Jerusalem attending a feast. Philip went up to the man and asked him if he understood what he was reading. The Ethiopian answered, "How can I, unless someone instructs me?" He then invited Philip to join him in his journey.

As Philip and the Ethiopian traveled, Philip explained to him the meaning of Isaiah's words. He showed how Isaiah's prophecies had been fulfilled in Jesus Christ. As they traveled, they came to a place were there was some water. The Ethiopian asked Philip why he could not be baptized. Philip answered that if he believed he could be baptized. When the treasurer answered that he did believe that Jesus was the Son of God, Philip baptized him. The Ethiopian continued his journey filled with joy and the Holy Spirit. (This man went home where he most likely was the first person to spread the Gospel message among the Ethiopian people.)

The Conversion of Saul

The history of the Catholic Church is filled with stories of remarkable conversions. Though every conversion is of infinite spiritual value, most have no discernible impact upon history. Yet, there are a select few men and women who are called by God in moments of crisis in the Church. These men and women are called to a special vocation to change the very course of history. Joan of Arc and Ignatius of Loyola are two such examples. However, the greatest of all the saints to be called by God in a moment of crisis was the Church's greatest persecutor.

Philip baptizes the Ethiopian.

After the martyrdom of St. Stephen, there was no more active persecutor of the Christian Church than Saul. Though a sinner, Saul was not an evil man. He was, in fact, quite rare. He was a man of total personal and intellectual honesty. He hunted the Christians because he honestly believed they were God's enemies.

Determined to kill all the Christians that he could get his hands on, Saul went to the High Priest. He asked the High Priest for letters of introduction to the synagogues in Damascus. Saul wanted the letters so that he could go to Damascus and arrest the Christians he found there and bring them back to Jerusalem.

Filled with a steely determination and armed with his letters, Saul set out for Damascus. As he neared the city, a bright light blazed out of Heaven all about him. He fell from his horse as though struck by lightning. From Heaven a voice boomed forth, "Saul, Saul! Why do you persecute Me?" Confused and dazed, Saul asked who spoke. The Voice answered, "I am Jesus, Whom you persecute." This exchange caused the most complete change ever wrought in any person.

Trembling, Saul asked what Jesus wanted him to do. Our Lord told Saul to go into Damascus where he would be told what to do next. Saul got off the ground and opened his eyes, but could not see. His companions led him to Damascus. For three days he lived at

Paul fell from his horse as though struck by lightning.

the house of a Christian man named Judas. Still blind, Saul did not eat or drink.

Meanwhile, living in Damascus at the time was a Christian named Ananias. God appeared to Ananias and told him to go to Saul at Judas' house. Our Lord told Ananias to lay his hands on Saul so that he would regain his sight. Ananias, who knew Saul's reputation, feared going to see him. However, Our Lord told Ananias that Saul was "a chosen instrument of Mine." With this assurance, Ananias went to see Saul.

As soon as Ananias placed his hands on Saul, his sight was restored. He stood up and Ananias baptized him. He would now be called by his Greek name, Paul. Paul ate and drank and regained his strength. He would need that strength, for it would carry him around the known world.

Paul Escapes Damascus

With the same relentless passion that Paul had used to attack the Church, he now went into the synagogues of Damascus and began to preach that Jesus was the Son of God. The Jews and Christians who heard him were amazed. They could not believe it was the same man who had killed the Christians in Jerusalem and come to Damascus to arrest them.

After a few weeks, Paul's preaching angered the Jews. They met and planned to kill him. However, Paul learned of their scheme. During the night, Paul's followers snuck him out of town by lowering him over the city walls in a basket. Paul fled into Arabia, where he spent the next year in prayer, preparing for his coming mission.

Chapter Review

Fill in the blanks to complete the sentences below.

1. Peter and John went to Samaria to _____ the men and women whom Philip had baptized.

2. One of the people Philip baptized was an important official from _____, who likely went home and spread the Gospel among his people.

3. Saul hunted Christians because _____.

4. As Saul neared _____, a bright light blazed out of Heaven all about him.

5. Paul escaped from Damascus one night, when his followers snuck him out of town by _____.

Chapter 29 — The Work of St. Peter

Peter baptizes Cornelius and his family.

Peter Brings the Gentiles into the Church

With Paul's conversion, the persecution of the Church decreased. The Church in Judea, Galilee, and Samaria was at peace. The numbers of Catholics increased.

During this time of peace, Peter traveled around Judea preaching, confirming, and working miracles. At Lydda, he cured a man named Aeneas who had been paralyzed for eight years. In Joppa, Peter raised a beloved widow named Tabitha from the dead. The news of these miracles spread all over the land and many people became Christians.

While Peter was staying in Joppa, messengers came to him from a Roman centurion named Cornelius. Though not a Jew, Cornelius was a good and holy man who had been attracted to the Jewish faith because of its high moral teaching. One day while he was praying, an angel had appeared to Cornelius. The angel told him that God had heard his prayers. The angel told Cornelius to send some men to Simon's house in Joppa, where they would find Peter. Peter would tell him what to do next. Cornelius immediately sent three messengers to Joppa.